Where Two Worlds Meet
How to Develop
Evidential Mediumship

by
Janet Nohavec

With
Suzanne Giesemann

Aventine Press

Published by Aventine Press
750 State Street #319
San Diego CA, 92010

www.aventinepress.com

Library of Congress Control Number: 2010918119
Library of Congress Cataloging-in-Publication Data
Where Two Worlds Meet How to Develop Evidential Mediumship

ISBN: 1-59330-697-0
Printed in the United States of America

Contents

PART III – MAKING CONTACT

APPENDICES

Acknowledgements

To my parents, who never got to dance in this lifetime.
To my family, whose support shines through our collective trials:
Thank you.
To my nieces: Live bravely. Sing your song.
To my friends: Life wouldn't be as rich without you.
To the girls: Your support was incredible.
To my church: Peace and love.
To our benefactor — our angel: My heartfelt gratitude for believing in me.
To my students: If you serve humanity and the spirit world,
I have taught you well.
To Suzanne — my author: Your poetry, integrity, and gift shine brightly.
To Joseph — Thank you for the artwork.
To God, the angels, saints, and departed loved ones:
I have loved painting you back to life.
To my fellow mediums of integrity: Thank you for standing.
Mediumship is a gift from God - treat it as such
For all the hands that held me up when walking wasn't easy: Thank you.
Hum though life. Sing your song.
Bring light to all darkness.
Never, never, never give up, nor give an inch.
Like a lighthouse, shine for all to see God's light in you.

Introduction

The first time I saw a spirit person I ran screaming for my mother. Of course, by the time I dragged her back to the garage where I'd seen the scary man, he was gone. My detailed description of his gaunt face, his dark hair and goatee, and his black suit, hat, and shoes matched the grandfather I'd never met. My mother was a very superstitious woman, so my seeing her dead father-in-law in the garage was not a good thing.

With an abusive, alcoholic father, my childhood was anything but happy and peaceful. So when my grandfather showed up later at my bedside, I wanted no part of him. He started bringing my grandmother along—perhaps to comfort me after one of my father's drunken rages—but their presence only terrified me. The grand extent of our one-sided conversations consisted of me begging them to go away.

Thankfully, they listened. I didn't see any spirit people again until I was well into my twenties. By then I was living in a convent run by the Sisters of Charity. I may have suppressed my ability to see spirits, but a few years earlier I'd been awakened in the middle of the night by a voice clearly telling me that I was going to be a Catholic nun. It was my turn to listen, and unable to ignore what I then perceived as a *calling*, I took my first vows.

It was there in the convent that the spirits started to show up again. The men and women in the paintings on the walls would talk to me, telling me their life stories. I saw long-deceased nuns walking around the cemetery. I chalked it all up to the spiritual atmosphere I was immersed in: Catholic saints had been talking to spirits for centuries; it seemed only natural that I would hear and see them, too, in that kind of environment.

I'd given up all of my possessions to become a nun, but after five years I decided I could serve God better on the outside. After some of the most difficult soul searching of my life, I left the convent and took a management job at a Catholic retreat center. It was then, on one of my days off, that I had a chance encounter with a medium. That event altered the course of my life and changed my entire belief system.

I soon learned that being able to sense the presence of spirit people was a gift, not something to fear. Once I began to honor my abilities, I discovered that I could use my gifts to heal others. Since then, I've traveled the world to develop and expand my mediumistic powers. I've worked with police and families on missing persons cases. I've given readings for people in 30 countries. I've been featured in dozens of news stories and articles and have appeared on live television and radio.

My mother once asked me, "Janet, how can you go from being a nun to talking to dead people?"

As I explained to her, it's all about living a life of service. I served others as a nun, and I continue to help others now as a medium and as an ordained Spiritualist minister. I went from being Sister Janet to Reverend Nohavec, pastor of my own church, *The Journey Within.* It's a privilege and an honor to connect those who once walked this earth with those who are still here. It's an incredible feeling to touch the hem of the next world. The spirit people never fail to leave me as breathless as my clients at the evidence they give us from the other side that life is continuous.

I've always believed that whatever you do, you should do it well. If not, why do it at all? I've applied that philosophy to everything I've ever done in my life, but never to anything so vital as my current work. As a medium, it's my job to build a bridge between this world and the next.

And that's not something you do halfway.

This book—as the title says—is about talking to the spirit world, which is what mediums do. A medium serves as the intermediary between those of us souls still walking around in a physical body and those who've shed their body during the transition we call death. We reunite family members with loved ones they thought were gone forever.

In the pages that follow, I'm going to teach you how to practice a very specific kind of mediumship: *evidential* mediumship. Look up *evidence* in the dictionary, and you'll see words like *proof, verification*, and *substantiation*, which is exactly what clients want from a medium. But let me be clear from the start: I don't try to prove anything to anyone. I simply do my best to provide an overwhelming body of evidence that I'm communicating with the other side.

The spirit people also want the mediums they work with to be credible. Think about it: They've waited all this time to talk to their loved ones through you … Why would they just give you a psychic message? They want your client to be convinced that they've paid them a visit, and that's not going to happen from a medium who says, "Your Mother's here, and she says you're gonna win a million bucks."

It's all about the evidence.

How do you convince someone that you're talking to their dead father or mother? You pass along details and messages from the other side that you, as the medium, had no earthly way of knowing. That's evidence, and as far as I'm concerned, it's the only way to practice mediumship.

My church was made possible because I'm an evidential medium. I started out leading services in the back room of a bookstore. I couldn't have bought the building where we now meet were it not for the generosity of one of my clients. That man—a lifelong Catholic who had lost his child—never would have helped me if I'd given him a psychic message. Never. He helped me because I brought his deceased daughter back to him during several very evidential readings. I passed along memories from his child that no one but she and his family could have known.

The man's wife said that a reading with me was like a phone call from Heaven. And that's what I do. For a few precious minutes I paint people back to life with my words, and I won't settle for anything less than a verbal masterpiece every time.

If you want to be a credible medium, neither should you.

When you paint someone back to life, you talk about the clothes they used to wear, right down to Uncle Harry's funny bow ties or the pink ribbons Aunt Martha always used to put in her hair. You describe a photo that's sitting on your client's dresser at home, or you mention their mother's favorite song.

At this point you may be thinking, *That sounds like hard work.* And it is! My goal is to wow myself with my accuracy at every reading and public demonstration I give. I aim to amaze my clients, too, but not because I want to put on a great show. This is not about showmanship. It's not about personal gain. This is sacred, spiritual work. It's about bringing comfort to those left behind by showing that life is continuous. It's about demonstrating that death is merely a transition, and not a thing to be feared. It's about helping people to get on with their lives until they meet their loved ones again.

The other day I gave a demonstration of mediumship at the end of one of my classes. I brought through the father of a female student named Pat. The man showed himself and spoke to me very clearly.

"Why's he talking about St. Patrick's Day?" I asked Pat. She gave a crooked smile and said, "My dad wanted a boy, so he always called me *Patrick* instead of *Patricia*."

I never could have guessed such a thing, so to me, that was a "hit"—evidential, but not a home run yet. I gave her several other bits of information to prove to her that I was really communicating with her father. Pat nodded in understanding with every accurate detail. Then, as the reading came to a close, I hit a grand slam as I watched the man pantomime what seemed to be an important message for his daughter.

"He keeps shoving something in my shirt pocket," I said, mimicking the gesture by putting something in my imaginary breast pocket as he did it.

Pat wiped at her tears as she let the class in on a secret: She had written a letter to her father just after he died. In it, she told him all the things she never got to say to him while he was alive. Unbeknownst to anyone—especially not to me—she had slipped the letter into his shirt pocket at the funeral as he lay in his coffin.

"Well," I told my stunned student as her father smiled in the background, "your dad got that letter."

And *that's* what I mean by evidence. That woman will never again doubt that her father is still around her. She now knows that he'll be there to greet her when she crosses over.

The implications of an evidential reading like that are astounding. Pat may have thought her letter went with her father to the grave unread, but now she knows better. Now she and everyone who was in my class that day know in their hearts that our loved ones are aware of our actions … and of our love.

Unfortunately, evidential mediumship is becoming a lost art. These days, too many mediums settle for giving less than evidence. Way less. And that's unacceptable, because there's a tremendous responsibility that goes along with this work. There's no way you're going to convince others of the continuity of life by telling a client, "I have your grandmother here from the other side, and she wants you to know that she loves you."

Where's the evidence in that?

Giving fluffy, non-evidential messages is taking the easy way out. It gives mediumship a bad name. It opens the door for frauds and charlatans, and it provides ammunition to the skeptics. You could turn blue in the face trying to convince a skeptic that our work is real, but a medium's job is to allow people to have a personal experience of the next world. That's what changes people.

Mediumship is not a psychic sideshow. In a field that's already full of pitfalls, you have to stand on a rock of integrity. Nothing else is acceptable. There's a much bigger implication to all of this than merely astounding others. We are dealing with intelligence on the other side—living, functioning minds that know what they're doing and know what we're doing as well. The spirit world has access to knowledge, information, and guidance that's unavailable to most people on the earth plane. The spirit people can help us not only to heal ourselves and our clients ... they can help our planet to evolve.

But if they're going to help us, we have to listen to them. And we have to be credible. By becoming a medium, you're taking on important work, but you're also taking a risk. It's not easy to sit in front of a client in a private reading or stand before a crowd of strangers in a public demonstration and pass along messages that only you are privy to. You open yourself up to embarrassment and criticism. So why do it?

You do it because the gift of mediumship is part of your uniqueness. It's a gift that God has given you, and that's not something you waste. We provide a rare and awe-inspiring service not just to our fellow human beings, but to the spirit world as well. The spirit people are counting on you just as much as your clients are. Evidential mediums are few and far between. The spirit world needs you to be their connection with their loved ones—to get the message across that they're still around and that love never dies—and we cannot let them down.

If it sounds like I take this work seriously, you're right. I do what I do because I believe in it with all my heart, and so should you.

In this book I'm going to teach you how to identify and develop your unique mediumistic gifts. But first, I want you to choose what kind of medium you want to be. Clients know the difference between evidential and psychic messages. If you want to change people's lives with your messages from the other side, then read on, and choose the evidential way.

PART I

THE BASICS

Chapter 1

The Spirit World

Most people have the same questions about the spirit world. They want to know what happens when we die. They want to know where we go from here. They wonder what Heaven is like, and they desperately want to know if we'll be reunited with those we've loved and lost.

I'll answer all of these questions and more in the coming pages, but from someone who has talked to countless spirits who once walked the same ground we do, let me give you the short answer to the most pressing ones right up front: Of course life continues after we die, and yes, love goes on forever. This life is not all there is. The material plane where we live is just one level. There's a lot more to the world than meets the eye. A whole lot more.

We live in a world of physical matter: of hard things and soft things that get in our way. Like all material objects, our bodies appear solid to us because our physical senses perceive them as solid. But actually, if you examine the atoms of supposedly solid objects microscopically, you'll find that they're mostly empty space anyway.

Quantum physicists now tell us that everything in the universe is energy, vibrating at different frequencies, including you and me. We can see and feel an ice cube because its electrons vibrate at a slow enough speed that to us, it seems solid. Liquid water is made of the same particles as an ice cube, only the particles in the water vibrate faster, so it feels less solid than the ice. Speed those particles up even more and the water turns to vaporous steam. We can feel humidity in the air, but we can't see it. Does that mean it isn't there?

There are radio waves and cell phone conversations zipping past our ears this very moment. The only reason we can't hear them is because they're vibrating too fast. Our bodies are unable to tune in to such high frequencies. We have to use a radio or a cell phone to pick up those signals.

Think about the blades of an electric fan. When the fan is turned off, we can clearly see the blades. When the fan is turned on, they go around so fast that we can't see them anymore, but I guarantee if you stuck your hand in there you'd be convinced that they exist!

Because we're physical beings, our beliefs about the nature of reality tend to be anchored in our five physical senses. For hard-core materialists, if they can't see things, hear them, feel them, taste them, or smell them, they doesn't exist—which is kind of like the men back in Columbus's day who were sure the great explorer was going to sail right off the edge of the horizon. These days, explorers into other realms know that just because most people can't see or hear spirits doesn't mean they're not there.

There's something in a medium's "wiring" that allows us to tune into the higher vibration of spirits—to be the receiver and transmitter for those people in the physical world who can't perceive the spirit world's frequency. This special gift allows us access to the answers to some of the most important questions we'll ask in our lifetimes.

The information that follows comes both from my personal experience in communicating with the spirit world and from the archives of spirit readings for well over a century, starting with the birth of modern Spiritualism in 1848. Since then, many prominent men and women have dedicated their lives to psychical research. Many, such as Judge John W. Edmonds, a Chief Justice of the New York Supreme Court, Dr. Robert Hare, a retired University of Pennsylvania professor, and Reverend William Stainton Moses, an Anglican minister and English Master at University College began investigating mediumship to prove that it was fraudulent. All came to accept it as real and became dedicated Spiritualists.

The most interesting part about comparing the archives of mediumistic readings is the similarities in the messages mediums have brought through from the other side. Back when Spiritualism was in its infancy, mediums couldn't share their stories like we can today. The fact that the historical data provides such similar descriptions of the other side without any collaboration among the mediums gives further credibility to our understanding of life after death and what actually happens when we die.

Not just individuals have conducted research into life after death, but respected organizations and universities, as well. In the late 1800s the Cambridge Society for Psychical Research was formed to investigate the work of mediums. This became the forerunner for the respected Society for Psychical Research of London, organized by some of Britain's most eminent scholars and scientists. In the 1950s, medium Estelle Roberts helped the Spiritualist movement gain official recognition from the British government when she demonstrated her mediumistic abilities before the House of Commons. Mediumship today is widely accepted in the United Kingdom, where members of royalty, including some of the British queens in the past had their own, private mediums.

In the United States, Abraham Lincoln attended at least one séance held at the White House with medium Nettie Colburn and traveled to Georgetown for one of Nettie's circles. Medium Leonora Piper used her gifts to convince Professor William James of Harvard University about the reality of communication with the other side. He went on to found the American Society for Psychical Research.

In more recent years in the U.S., highly respected schools and organizations such as Duke University's Rhine Center continue to investigate paranormal phenomena and parapsychology. At the University of Arizona, Dr. Gary Schwartz, professor of psychology, neurology, medicine, psychiatry, and surgery has conducted scientific experiments into life after death, bringing together some of the top mediums in the country. His work continues today as part of the VERITAS program, whose aim is to discover the truth about the survival of consciousness and the continuity of life.

Data from studies such as these at universities, from psychical research societies, and from reputable mediums for more than a century all provide answers to the most commonly asked questions such as:

Where do we go from here?

A discussion of this topic conveys one of the most important messages that mediums have to offer: Death is merely a transition to another phase of our eternal existence. It's a doorway through that thin veil that separates us from the unseen world.

All matter is temporary. Everything physical eventually deteriorates and decays. Lucky for us, we're more than our physical bodies. Inside our shell of skin and bones we are all spiritual beings made of pure energy, as

I mentioned before. Scientists have proven that energy can be converted, but never destroyed, and that holds true for our spirit, which is eternal. We don't just *have* a spirit: we *are* spirits, temporarily housed in a temporary body.

Right now we have a physical body, but we also have a spiritual body that is the mirror image of the one we see. That spirit body goes with us when we die, as do our mind and our personality. The only thing that's different after our heart beats for the final time is that we are no longer clothed in skin and bones. Otherwise, nothing changes! The "you" that you know, the "I" that began at the moment of your conception, will continue into eternity.

If you have trouble grasping that thought, think about this: How did you feel when you were 10 years old? How did you feel when you were 20? Did you look at older people back then and think that they somehow felt different than younger people? How do you feel at your present age? Gradually, as the years pass, we come to discover that we may grow wiser, but we don't feel any different mentally as we age, no matter how old we get. That's because we are not our bodies. Our brain, organs, muscles, and other physical parts may slow down and deteriorate, but the spirit is eternal. It's the part of us that doesn't change as we age. It's that constant unwavering awareness that we exist—the part of us that says, *I am.*

The spirit realm is just as real to the spirit people as the physical realm is to those of us in physical bodies, only it's a realm of pure vibration ... pure energy ... pure awareness. The physical obstacles of our world don't obstruct the spirit people because just like x-rays that go right through solid matter, spirits vibrate at a much higher frequency than we do. They can move right through all that empty space in the atoms that make up our physical matter with no problem. To them, it's a world without things that go bump.

But here's the thing: *It's all the same world.*

The spirit world is not "out there" somewhere, just as Heaven isn't "up there" in the clouds. Their world is our world, only most people don't realize this because they can't perceive the spirit world. The "other side" is merely the other side of a micro-thin veil that envelopes us and clouds our current perceptions. The spirit world is a realm of pure thought—a world where time and space have no meaning. Death is merely a transition from the physical realm to the spiritual realm, which we've already said is intermingled with our own.   Death is a change in consciousness, in awareness, and in attunement to an environment where our minds are now able to perceive vibrations that they couldn't perceive with physical eyes.

Think about it. Right now every object we see appears to us in a range of colors from red to violet. Those colors are nothing more than vibrations of light at a specific frequency on the electro-magnetic scale that our eyes are attuned to perceive . So, what if our eyes were fine-tuned a bit? Science has proven that the electro-magnetic scale extends below and far above the range at which we perceive the rays. What would we see if we could step up the attunement of our eyes? Those higher frequency waves would reveal colors we can't even imagine right now only because we don't have the proper equipment to detect them.

If we could increase our mind's attunement to the higher vibrations of the spirit world, we would be able to experience what they do. Luckily, mediums are able to tune in part-way to their world and thus perceive thoughts and images from those now living on the other side.

What happens when we die?

Our spirit is the force that animates our body. It's the force that causes us to take each breath and that keeps our heart beating. When the body is no longer useful to the spirit, whether that results from a tragic accident or from the normal process of aging, the spirit is no longer attached to the body. The physical part of us eventually decays, but the "I am" awareness of the spirit continues to exist after our final heartbeat.

The spirit people have told me that the moment of death is an overwhelmingly positive and loving experience. Happily, none of the spirits that have communicated with me or with any other medium throughout history has ever mentioned a painful death. There may have been pain due to illness in the moments leading up to death, but once the transition is inevitable, it is always peaceful.

I once gave a reading to a man whose younger brother came through to me from the spirit world. The spirit-brother showed me quite vividly that he had died in a fiery car crash. I had no way of knowing this, but I knew from my client's reaction that my detailed description of that tragic event was right on the mark.

The man's family had been tormented for years with the thought that he'd died engulfed in flames. During the reading, the younger brother told me how the spirit people, knowing it was his time, came and escorted him to the other side before he could suffer. Having given my client irrefutable evidence that I was actually communicating with his brother, I was then able to comfort him with the news that his brother had felt no pain or torment as he left his body. The younger brother told me himself that his spirit was already on its way to the other side when the flames reached him.

The spirit people almost always tell me of being met by loved ones who had crossed over before them or by a guardian angel or angels who had been watching over them while they were still in physical form. No one arrives without a proper greeting, and all are engulfed in a blissful feeling of overwhelming love and acceptance. The loss of a loved one may be painful for those left behind, but it's not at all tragic for the one who leaves.

Shortly after our arrival on the other side we go through a review of our life. Like watching a movie in fast-forward, we're shown all of the good and bad deeds we performed while in physical form. The purpose of this life review is not to pass judgment, but to recognize those times when we failed to be loving and kind. We realize that our time on the physical earth was given to us for the purpose of learning, experiencing, developing our character, and progressing ever closer to God in our ability to love. After this review, decisions are made as to the best way for us to continue to grow spiritually while in this new phase of our existence ... while in the so-called Heaven.

What is Heaven Like?

Many Spiritualists refer to Heaven as the *Summerland,* for that's how it appears to the spirits who have crossed over. If you think of our planet on a beautiful summer day, you're on the right path, but I've been shown that it's even more beautiful than that.

Heaven is a different dimension of reality—a different state of mind, so to speak—but it's also a place. In a way, it's like the world of your dreams at night, complete with "things" such as trees, flowers, and even buildings and schools ... all of them seemingly very real to the one having the dream, but all of them created by mere thought.

So the other side is a world of thought, not matter. Those who have crossed over don't need words to talk with one another, they communicate telepathically. Their mode of transportation is also thought. If they want to visit Aunt Mary in Pittsburgh, they simply think of being at her side, and instantly they're there. They can be anywhere in our world in an instant because they inhabit a plane where time and space don't exist—only thought.

Spirits don't need a body to get around, but they maintain an ethereal body which mirrors the one they had while in physical form. In spite of whatever handicaps or infirmities they might have had while on the earth plane, once in Heaven, spirits find themselves with a perfect spirit body at the age when they were most vital. Because spirits can manipulate things with their thoughts, they can appear to a medium at whatever age would be recognizable to their loved ones, complete with clothes, glasses, or other familiar possessions such as a cane or wheelchair, which they no longer need on the other side.

Because of the higher and more refined vibrations of their world, the spirit people tell us of colors so beautiful that artists on our earth could never depict them. They tell us they have flowers more beautiful and fragrances that pale in comparison with those in the physical world. No longer limited by the physical body, the spirit people are free of pain, free to go where they want, to turn their thoughts into reality. No longer worried about money or food, there's no greed, no selfishness, no unemployment. All gifts and abilities are used in service to others.

The spirit people tell us that death is only a tragedy to those left behind. We only really begin to live when we die.

Will we be united with those we've loved and lost?

You can count on it. Over and over the spirit people tell me that they were met upon their arrival by those they wanted most to see, and they will be there for us when it's our time to cross over, too. Those of us on the earth plane still have lessons to learn while we're here, so it may seem like an eternity to wait until we're reunited again. Those on the other side live in a realm where time doesn't mean the same thing to them as it does to us. They watch us with love, knowing we'll see each other in what to them is the blink of an eye.

Do they hear us when we talk to them?

Absolutely. They see you kissing their picture, too. And they read the letters and poems you write for them. They're there at the graduation ceremonies, the weddings, and all the other special events you cry at because you think they missed out on. But you don't need to cry, because they come through very clearly during my sessions and tell me that they're often around us more in spirit than they ever were when they were in physical form. So tell your clients to keep on kissing their pictures. To talk to them. Believe me, they're listening, and they're always glad to hear from us.

There are two things we're guaranteed in this life: We're born and we die. No one escapes the final journey. But knowing what we now know about the other side, the implications of our time on this earth and what follows are life-changing. What we do here truly matters. Those who have not made the most of their lifetime will come face to face with their behavior, and there will be ramifications. The phrase, "You reap what you sow" is not only true; it should be the guiding principle behind every action we take each moment.

There is ultimate justice for our deeds on earth, for we ascend to the level on the other side that we earned while here in physical form. You don't suddenly become more spiritual just because you're a spirit without a body. Your soul continues to grow while on the next spiritual plane. The goal is to continue ever upward toward God, so that eventually we don't ever have to return to the earth.

If you, as a student of mediumship, are interested in further research into this field, I highly recommend any of the books by Andrew Jackson Davis, most especially *Nature's Divine Revelation* and *Harmonial Philosophy*. Often referred to as the father of Modern Spiritualism, his information about the afterlife, or "the Summerland," as he referred to the next plane of existence, will provide you with valuable insight.

Perhaps one of the most beautiful books ever written about the other side is *The Life Beyond the Veil*, which includes spirit messages received and written down by Reverend G. Vale Owen, an Anglican priest. This book has a foreword by Sir Arthur Conan Doyle, author of the Sherlock Holmes mysteries. Conan Doyle was an ardent supporter of Spiritualism and conducted extensive research into the field of mediumship. He documented the various planes of existence in his highly respected book, *The History of Spiritualism*.

With all of this background about the spirit world, it should now be clear how vital a medium's role is. Not only do we comfort others with the message that there is no death, but we remind people about the importance of taking personal responsibility and being accountable for their actions. Perhaps even more important, we provide a voice for the spirit world.

Communication with the other side is two-way. The spirit people want to talk with us as badly as we want to talk with them. Just as I mentioned in the introduction, we must always remember that when we pierce through that unseen veil, we're dealing with intelligence—with living entities who long to work with us and guide us. By helping us along our spiritual path, they further their own growth as well as ours.

With that in mind, let's talk about this wondrous work of ours ...

Chapter 2
What is Mediumship?

The year was 1425. The place: the village of Domremy, France. A thirteen year old girl, the daughter of a peasant farmer, was working in the family garden when she saw a brilliant light and clearly heard a voice speaking to her. For the next two years she continued to hear ever more insistent voices and saw the figures of saints and angels. The voices gradually let the girl know that they were communicating with her for a reason: she had been chosen to save her country.

That girl was Joan of Arc. In spite of her father's disbelief and ridicule, Joan informed the local authorities that she had been told to go to the aid of King Charles. When everyone merely laughed at her, Joan returned home and told the voices that she was a poor girl who wasn't cut out to ride or fight. The voices answered back, "It is God who commands it!"[1]

Joan of Arc went on to lead the French in their siege on the city of Orleans, but she was eventually taken prisoner and condemned as a witch and a heretic. The courts finally determined that Joan had, in fact, heard the voices of spirits. Unfortunately, their decision came 25 years after she had been set on fire in a public square for her "false and diabolical visions."[2] The French recognized their mistake and went on to make Joan a national hero, even naming a holiday in her honor. The Catholics later made her a saint. She now stands for the entire world as a symbol of the integrity and the deep sense of purpose that would allow a person to die for what they believed in.

1 http://www.newadvent.org/cathen/08409c.htm
2 http://www.newadvent.org/cathen/08409c.htm

Joan of Arc heard voices and saw spirits. Hundreds of thousands of sensitive people before and after her also were aware of people from the spirit world and were burned or drowned because of their gift. Were they and Joan of Arc mediums? To answer that question, we first have to define some terms ...

What is mediumship?

Mediumship is a form of communication between physical human beings and discarnate spirits. It is a way of relaying information between two levels of reality that requires cooperation on both sides. Mediums, because of their special attunement to the vibrations of the spirit world, become the instruments through which the spirit people touch our world. Mediumship erects a bridge between the physical and the non-physical.

Mental Mediumship

There are two types of mediumship: mental and physical. Mental mediumship involves the transmission of information through the vibration of thought, rather than through the five senses. Thought may be intangible to us, but it has its own energy which is transferred through focused consciousness. Depending on the abilities of the individual, a medium receives information from the spirit world through any or all of the following mental methods:

Clairvoyance

Clairvoyance is the ability to see a spirit or the images that are sent telepathically by a spirit. The word has its roots in two French words: *claire* (clear) and *voir* (to see), so clairvoyance literally means "clear seeing." Unfortunately, the images a medium sees clairvoyantly are not always as clear as the word implies.

I'm often able to see a spirit the same way I see a living person. I see them in the room with me. This type of seeing is a rare gift and is known as objective clairvoyance. The most common way mediums see clairvoyantly is through subjective clairvoyance, which is much like the way we see things in our imagination—as mental images.

Clairaudience

If clairvoyance is "clear seeing," then the root word *audio* in clairaudi-ence should give this one away. Mediums who are clairaudient are able to *hear* messages from the spirit world. True clairaudience occurs when a medium hears the actual voice of the spirit outside his or her own body, which is known as objective clairaudience. Not all mediums hear the ac-tual spirit voices. Many times clairaudient messages come across just like the medium's own thoughts in what is called subjective clairaudience.

Clairsentience

By now you should be able to figure out from the root of the word that *clairsentience* is the ability to *sense* or feel information from the spirit world. Clairsentience can be used to sense the height, size, and stature of the spirit communicator. It can include sensing scents or odors that trigger memories for your sitter.

Inspired writing

Inspired writing occurs when a person writes words and thoughts re-ceived from the spirit world. The letters are written in the medium's own handwriting, but the ideas come from the spirits themselves. This differs from automatic writing, a form of physical mediumship in which the spirit communicator directs the movement of the medium's hand.

When inspired by spirit, the writer makes no effort to put words to-gether—the thoughts simply come to mind. Rather than consciously fo-cusing on what to write, it's like taking dictation and simply writing down what you hear or sense. Often, the thoughts come in bursts of "knowing" and are translated by the medium into words that have meaning to others.

St. John of the Cross was a Spanish mystic and priest in the 16th cen-tury who was imprisoned for trying to reform the Carmelite order. While isolated in a tiny cell, and later after being freed, St. John wrote poetry that earned him recognition as one of the foremost poets in the Spanish lan-guage. While I wouldn't technically call St. John a medium (in that I don't think he was talking to dead people), I do feel strongly that he was com-municating with higher intelligence. Much of the information he wrote about the spiritual mountain that we climb was given to him from saints and angels through inspired writing.

Trance

Trance mediumship occurs when a spirit communicator shares the consciousness of a medium. In the four types of mental mediumship described above, the medium remains fully aware of the spirit communications coming from the other side. In trance mediumship, the spirit's consciousness often overshadows the medium's consciousness along a range from a light trance state to the point where the medium may not be aware of what she or he is saying or doing.

Contrary to popular belief, in no case does the medium completely surrender control of their mind. In trance mediumship, there is cooperation between the medium and the spirit world. The spirits never control us. It is a blending of consciousness, but deep somnambulistic states are only for those who have an extensive knowledge of this type of work. Trance mediumship requires years to develop and should be taken very seriously. Even for those born with the potential for trance mediumship, the unfoldment of this gift should be done under the tutelage of someone with experience in this subject.

All mediumship involves an altered state of consciousness. Trance, in itself, is used for different reasons. The depth and level of trance determines whether it is being used in a light state for evidential mediumship or for work such as discovering greater wisdom and philosophical ideas, which would involved a complete overshadowing of the medium's consciousness.

My first trance experience occurred just after I left the convent. While I had been seeing spirits off and on my whole life, I didn't really understand what was happening and I knew nothing about mediumship. I was invited to participate in a psychic development circle in the back room of a bookstore owned by an old friend. I had no idea what to expect when I joined the group of twelve open-minded people sitting in a circle of chairs.

I closed my eyes and noticed that my heart was beating faster than normal. I chalked that up to nervousness at the thought of the others staring at me. Then I started to get dizzy, as if the room were spinning. I felt a strange buzzing throughout my body and saw wonderful, sparkly lights dancing behind my eyelids.

I have to admit that the whole experience shook me up a bit. I told the others that I didn't know what was going on. The leader of the group advised me to simply let it flow and go with whatever was happening, so I did. The energy pulsing through my body made my arms and legs tremble, but I hung in there, and suddenly I became aware of the presence of a small woman in a purple dress. She was surrounded by a blindingly bright light. My ears roared with words I could barely make out other than what I understood to be the name *Maroni.*

While some people lose all awareness in a trance state, I could hear the group encouraging me to stay with it. I don't know how long the trance lasted, but just when I felt I couldn't take much more of the swirling and shaking, the woman and the sparkly lights vanished.

Keep in mind that this was my first experience with trance, and that none of the others in the room were experienced enough with trance to understand the situation any more than I could. I was frightened only because of the newness of the sensations. The sparkly lights and strong energy weren't dangerous, and the woman in purple very clearly came to me with love.

In the days and months that followed my first trance experience, I realized that Maroni was a spirit guide. I learned to contact her at will while in a light trance state. She showed me symbols that I intuitively sensed were meant to heal people. Other days she would share her philosophy about God. I wrote down the things she shared with me, and those writings could be classified as a form of automatic writing.

I hesitate to make a separate section here about channeling, but it needs mentioning to clear up some misconceptions. Channeling is a phenomenon in which a spirit communicates through a medium. The spirit may use a person's vocal cords, automatic writing, or use other means to communicate.

There have been some great channeled pieces such as the *Seth* books by Jane Roberts, or *A Course in Miracles*, in which Jesus is said to have spoken through psychologist Helen Schucman, and the popular words of the spirit Abraham, speaking through Esther Hicks. The information conveyed in these and other works is often wise and thought-provoking, and it shows excellent cooperation between higher intelligence and those of us on earth. I have to say, though, that although valuable, channeling has little to do with evidential mediumship because there is no validation that one is communicating with a dead relative.

Unfortunately, most of the so-called channeling that I have witnessed is not credible. Much of it is flowery, showy, and reflects a state of consciousness of the channeler's own mind. It does not come from a source of intelligence, and it is not mediumship. Trance mediums such as Andrew Jackson Davis, Emma Hardinge Britten, and Judith Seaman are reputable mediums who channel verifiable intelligence. Their work speaks for itself.

Physical Mediumship

Physical mediumship is an attempt from the spirit world to prove the continuity of life in an even more evidential manner than through strictly mental means. It occurs when the spirit people work through a medium to manipulate objects on the earth. It involves the transformation or manipulation of energy in such a way that events occur which are noticeable to humans through our five physical senses. Examples of physical mediumship include automatic writing, apports (things that seem to appear "out of nowhere"), table tipping, transfiguration, materialization, direct voice phenomena, and rapping.

If you mention rapping, most people who are familiar with the Spiritualist movement in the United States think of the Fox sisters. The two worlds have been communicating since Biblical times, but Modern Spiritualism pins its beginnings in the mid-1800s when Kate, Leah, and Margaret Fox claimed to be communicating with a spirit in their Hydesville, New York, house. The girls would ask the spirit questions, and it would respond with audible raps according to a code the sisters devised. The answers revealed not just a series of disjointed words, but the fact that the sisters were dealing with a source of intelligence. Many people tried to expose the Fox sisters as frauds, but no one ever proved deceit on their part.

Practiced legitimately by gifted mediums, physical mediumship provides another way for the spirit world to prove to us that life is continuous. As much as I acknowledge physical mediumship, I have to say that true physical phenomena are rare. It was actually quite common in the first half of the twentieth century, when the irrefutable evidence from the spirit world was so strong that people flocked to Spiritualist churches. With the help of a gifted medium, people would sit in séances and hear the actual voice of their loved ones speaking to them from a few inches away from their ear. For some reason, this type of mediumship is hard to find these days.

Unfortunately, throughout the history of mediumship there have been many who have used the gullibility of the public and a darkened room to practice deception. These frauds have been exposed for the most part, but mediumship has carried their negative baggage ever since. In spite of its rarity and in spite of the baggage, I do give credence to many aspects of physical mediumship. I believe that when the conditions are just right—when you have the perfect combination of love and attunement between this side and the other—that physical manifestations are possible.

That's what we're striving for in my church, anyway: for a physical sign that the spirit world respects us tremendously for our efforts and that they know we respect them just as much. When that day comes, I honestly believe they're going to send us an apport, and for me, I'd love to get a rose. Every time I ask St. Theresa for a sign that I should or shouldn't do something, she sends me roses, so in my church we're waiting for that rose to fall from the sky.

We're also working for materialization and direct voice like the great medium Estelle Roberts, who is one of those who could produce the actual spirit voices in the room. I believe in my heart that someday we will achieve this kind of cooperation between the two planes of existence in my church.

In the meantime, I choose to focus on evidential mental mediumship, both in my classes and here in this book. I want the words that come from your mouth to overwhelm others with the evidence that life is eternal and to leave no doubt in others' minds as to the source of that evidence.

* * *

Not all mediums are capable of all types of mediumship. Just as one person may have perfect hearing but needs glasses to see clearly, there are varying levels of skill with each type of sensing. A medium may be clairvoyant, clairaudient, and clairsentient, but one method of communication may be more prominent than another.

When I attended my first class at The Arthur Findlay College, the world's foremost school for the advancement of Spiritualism and psychic sciences in Stansted, England, I was given a form with the various types of mediumship listed. I had to describe my abilities by indicating which of the types of mediumship I had experienced. When my mentor, Nigel, saw that I had marked "yes" next to clairaudience, clairvoyance, clairsentience, and trance, I could tell by the look on his face that he didn't believe me.

Eighty students with varying levels of mediumistic gifts had shown up for the class. Nigel couldn't give personal attention to all eighty students, so he had a team of tutors to assist him. He chose me to be in his select group of students, sure that I was exaggerating my abilities. We butted heads more than a few times that first week (and in the many years since our close friendship began), but at the end of the course, Nigel had to admit that I was a natural born medium.

If you recognize that you have abilities in more than one type of mediumship, I recommend you determine which one is the strongest and work on developing that area first. Later you can work on the other areas, but one will always dominate.

What Mediumship is Not

Some people make the mistake of including mediumship with the New Age movement, which began in the 1960s and early 1970s. While the New Age movement started as a new kind of spirituality which combined eastern philosophies and metaphysical thought systems, today the term "New Age" has come to mean a mixture of anything-goes spirituality and practices. Unfortunately, some of these practices have no basis in fact and stray far from mediumship's principal goal of showing the continuity of life.

As I defined it earlier, mediumship is a form of communication between physical human beings and discarnate spirits. Mediumship requires a gifted and disciplined medium on the earth plane and the cooperation of those in the spirit world. Mediumship has been around since history began. It is not *new* and it is *not*:

Fortune telling. Back when I was 17, I visited an old babushka in New York City who sat behind a little table complete with crystal ball and tarot cards. The so-called fortune teller told me I was cursed and that I wouldn't find a boyfriend until I put the little pouch she gave me under my pillow. One month and 100 dollars later, I still wasn't de-cursed.

Yes, a medium can read the energy of a person and give psychic predictions, but I consider psychic predictions a part of seership, which is the ability to read the energy of time. Being a seer is a gift. It has nothing to do with street psychics or fortune tellers, nor is it something to be trivialized.

Palm reading. Palmistry, or reading a person's character and future based on the lines in a person's hands, is a fascinating art, but it has nothing to do with communication between the two worlds.

Astrology, numerology and card reading. These are all valid forms of divination, but they're not mediumship.

Mediumship is not entertainment. It's not about ego. It's not something you do to get rich, but mediums do have to earn a living. It does not involve playing on the grieving or making people dependent on what you have to tell them. It's not about power … it's about humility—because anyone who is given the ability to communicate with the other side can't help but be humbled.

Mediumship is not about accessing information that crosses a boundary, such as telling a client information of a sensitive nature. It's not about delving into deep emotional issues that would be better discussed in a private session with a psychologist.

And finally, mediumship has nothing to do with anything evil. It's not about "disturbing the dead," for the so-called dead people are very much "alive" except they're no longer bound by a physical body. As for disturbing them, they want to talk with us as much as we want to talk with them. The Spiritualists' philosophy is that there are no dead and there is no death.

* * *

I began this chapter with the story of Joan of Arc, who heard voices and saw the spirits of saints. Knowing what you know now, I'll ask the question again: Was Joan of Arc a medium? I say yes. Joan may not have had a name for what she saw or heard, but as I proved throughout my earlier life, you don't have to know you're a medium to be a medium.

I saw my grandfather's spirit as a child and the spirits of the dead nuns in the convent, but it wasn't until I learned what mediumship was that I realized I was practicing clairvoyance. If you're like me—a born medium—you may have been hearing, seeing, or sensing spirits all of your life, but for any number of reasons you downplayed your gifts. On the other hand, you may have never had a mediumistic experience in your life, but are interested in learning more and developing the ability to communicate with the other side.

This brings up a good question: Are mediums born or made? Some people will insist that anyone can be a medium. While I agree with that statement, I do believe that not everyone can be a great medium and that the best mediums are born. That having been said, if you have only come to realize your mediumistic abilities later in life, there's every reason to believe that you can develop them to a much greater degree. There is no limit to what a person can achieve with the proper focus, motivation, and dedication, and once you establish that magnetic link with the spirit world, the connection only grows stronger.

I've dedicated years of my life to studying and practicing my mediumship. When I first went to Stansted, England, and Nigel gave me a hard time, my first thought was "I don't need him!" As it turned out, I did, and I'm glad I stuck with him. Today, I tell my students the same thing Nigel told me back then: "Just give me 3-5 years ..."

In other words, this isn't something you learn overnight. It's not like a cup of instant soup where you just add hot water. Yes, I'm going to give you the ingredients you need to become a better medium, but it's you who has to do the hard work.

Joan of Arc took her work and the spirits' messages so seriously that she was willing to give up her life for what she believed. I'm not saying that you need to become a martyr for your mediumship, but I feel very strongly that we mediums need to take our work seriously. Just as when the saints spoke to Joan of Arc, the spirits on the other side may be trying to pass along important messages for our world today.

What if they're trying to talk to us now and no one is listening?

Chapter 3

Your Spiritual Self

When I began my work as a medium, I had no idea that so much pain existed on such a personal level for so many people. Each life has its individual losses, grief, and hardship, yet most of us walk around with our emotions bottled up inside. Loss is an inevitable part of this life. There's no way to avoid it. Part of our role as mediums is to help others to cope with their losses and their pain.

Everyone reacts differently to death. Some find it impossible to go on after the death of a loved one. Others, through the love and support of family and friends, begin to live again with a level of acceptance. As mediums, we can play a major role in helping a person to cope with loss by bringing back the love of one who has passed to the other side. We help by building that bridge of love and hope.

A person who doesn't understand the meaning of death and the afterlife can never fully understand this life and its most important implications. We help people come to that understanding. This role is the core of why we do this work, yet I've heard many mediums over the years talk about what a burden their talent has been. To those people I say, don't do it if you view it as a burden. Don't do us any favors! To be a medium is to be bestowed with a great treasure. You can't trivialize this work where we touch the hem of the spirit world.

All major religions believe in an afterlife, yet mediumship is not religious work … it's deeply spiritual work. How you fill in the blank on a form that asks what religion you are makes no difference when it comes to mediumship. Being religious means belonging to a particular organized group with a set of beliefs and traditions. Being spiritual is a way of life that involves a personal commitment to inner development and the search for ultimate meaning. To part the veil between the worlds and not believe in everlasting love has no meaning. All religions encourage us to talk to angels, saints, and God. Mediums simply add discarnate loved ones to that list.

Most people believe in God, but too few realize that life is a spiritual journey and that our role is to grow ever closer to God through love, kindness, and service while traveling along our individual paths. Those who wish to develop their psychic and mediumistic potential need to realize that along with the development of our gifts, we must develop spiritually. We must constantly attempt to come from a place of love, compassion, and grace, which are at the core of a spiritual life.

Albert Einstein had great suspicion against religious authority, yet he devoted a good deal of time pondering the mystery of conscious life. Regarding compassion for others, he said,

> "A human being is a part of the whole, called by us Universe, a part limited in time and space. He experiences himself, his thoughts and feelings as something separated from the rest—a kind of optical delusion of his consciousness. This delusion is a kind of prison, restricting us to our personal desires and to affection for a few persons nearest to us. Our task must be to free from this prison by widening our circle of compassion to embrace all living creatures and the whole nature in its beauty."[3]

God sent us here to grow individually, but collectively as well, by embracing all creatures, as Einstein said, and by helping each other. We make God present to the world through love and healing. Very few people realize the very sacredness of their being. If they did, we wouldn't have war or starvation. We would recognize that everyone is our brother because they were sent here by God.

Mother Teresa, who ministered to the poor, sick, and dying for over 45 years, treated all people with love and respect. She had the following quote on her wall in Calcutta, India:

---

3 http://www.special-dictionary.com/quotes/authors/a/albert_einstein/96271.htm

"People are unreasonable, illogical, and self-centered. Love them anyway. If you do good, people may accuse you of selfish motives. Do good anyway … The good you do today may be forgotten tomorrow. Do good anyway. Honesty and transparency make you vulnerable. Be honest and transparent anyway … People who really want help may attack you if you help them. Help them anyway. Give the world the best you have and you may get hurt. Give the world your best anyway."[4]

Mediums have a unique opportunity to serve humanity. Yes, we are open to attack from others whose belief systems restrict them. But as Mother Teresa advises, we do our work anyway. We are called to be a glowing light in the darkness of this world. When others suffer loss and become lost, we show them the way back to the light with love and compassion.

People who walk into my church comment on the tremendous feeling of love there. It's true. You can't help but feel the love in those walls, but there's also tremendous pain from all those who have lost a love one and come there wanting to know, "How do I go on?" We can't reverse their loss. We simply tell them, "We'll walk with you. We'll listen to you. We'll just hold you up if you need us to."

There's no magic in what we do. Beyond our mediumship, it's pure love and compassion. I've changed for the better each person who has sat across from me for a private session. For a short while I am invited into the world of another human being. People's hearts are fragile, but the human spirit is strong and love conquers all, even death.

Inside each of us is a God-given navigational system: call it your soul, your spirit, your conscience. We can't love one another and serve others without paying attention to that inner guidance. There are millions of people in this world who block out their spiritual side with greed and hate and fear. We need to let our light dispel the darkness, for that is why we're sent here: to manifest light and love and peace.

Before you can advance as a medium, you need to go inward and find the silence and peace that lies within. If you don't find peace there, you have some preliminary work to do. Most of us have obstacles to address, whether they come from family-of-origin problems or a lifetime of un-

4 http://prayerfoundation.org/mother_teresa_do_it_anyway.htm

healthy coping skills. Some of us may be selfish or egotistical, or we may need to work on being more patient, loving, or kind. Others may have addictions that need attention. Whatever the issue, it's impossible to advance our gifts to the highest possible degree unless we clean house first and get rid of our personal baggage.

I grew up in a highly dysfunctional family. I needed help to work past the problems that came from growing up in a loveless home with an abusive, alcoholic father. There's no shame in seeking professional help. We can't love others until we learn to love ourselves. The mediums, psychics, and seers I have respected the most have all made their personal growth as important as their spiritual growth, for both are intimately interrelated.

How do we bring the spiritual essence of God into our daily lives? Through prayer, meditation, and contemplation. All religious groups as well as the healing 12-step programs tell us to begin and end our day in prayer. Going within and spending time in silence is how we manifest God on Earth. We'll discuss meditation in a later chapter, but for now, know that meditation is listening to God and prayer is talking to God: displaying gratitude, asking for help, guidance, and inspiration.

Has God heard your voice lately?

Your spiritual development is as important as the development of your mediumistic gifts. The two go hand-in-hand. You can no more separate the two than you can separate the wave from the ocean. We are spiritual beings having a human experience. As such, we are temporarily away from our true spiritual home. If we don't take the time to be still, we can't hear the voice of God.

Have you talked to God today?

Did you take the time to listen?

As a medium, I believe in communicating with those who have crossed over. I also believe in communicating with all of the sources of guidance and help we can get, whether that be from God, from the saints, from angels, spirit guardians, or our deceased loved ones.

We may be the only person standing before a crowd to give a demonstration of mediumship, or the only person sitting in a room with grieving clients, but we never work alone. We are spiritual beings, intimately connected at the soul level both here and in the hereafter. If we want to improve our attunement with our inner guidance system and with all the souls waiting to help us, it's critical to make spiritual growth a priority.

I believe strongly that spending a lot of time in the presence of the energy of the recently departed must be balanced with a relationship with the higher realms of God or a strong interior spiritual discipline. Spending time in Nature can also provide balance for a medium. We are here to live out our own lives, balance is essential.

Chapter 4

Your Psychic Self

On the morning of December 26th, 2004, the animals along the coast of India and Sri Lanka began to behave strangely. Elephants raised their trunks, bellowed, and ran inland. Zoo animals rushed into their cages and refused to come back out. Flamingos fled their breeding areas and took to the sky along with swarms of bats. One man's dogs, who loved their daily run on the beach, refused to leave the house.

The two dogs saved the man's life, because shortly after these unusual displays of animal behavior, massive waves caused by an earthquake off the coast of northern Sumatra rolled ashore with devastating results. Ultimately 150,000 people lost their lives, but relatively few animals fell victim to what would be one of the deadliest tsunamis in history.

For centuries people have believed that animals possess a sixth sense. In recent years wildlife experts have claimed that it's the animals' acute attunement to the earth's vibrations that give them advance warning of natural phenomena such as earthquakes and tidal waves. And that's exactly what the sixth sense is: greater attunement to the energy and vibrations that we aren't normally aware of within the range our five physical senses.

Alan Rabinowitz, director for science and exploration at the Bronx Zoo Wildlife Conservation Society in New York, believes that humans also used to have this sixth sense but lost it when they no longer used it.[5] I believe that all of us still have our sixth sense, and that it will become more prominent when we regularly acknowledge and exercise it.

---

5 http://news.nationalgeographic.com/news/pf/16960960.html

The last chapter dealt with your spiritual self. This one is about your psychic self—the part of you that uses your non-physical senses to acquire information about the past, present, or future. In the 1930s this ability came to be known as extrasensory perception, or ESP, a term coined by J.B. Rhine, a researcher at Duke University.[6] Rhine considered telepathy, precognition, and clairvoyance to be aspects of ESP, but the term also includes what we now call the sixth sense, or simply a hunch, or intuition.

Throughout history, individuals have been singled out as having special psychic powers and foreseeing the future. Jesus knew Peter would betray him. Moses saw a symbolic burning bush. Nostradamus predicted major world events. Today, tens of thousands of students continue to follow the teachings and healing wisdom of American psychic Edgar Cayce.

While all of the individuals above and many more like them have been singled out for their extraordinary degree of gift, I believe that we all posses a psychic, intuitive side. How could we not, if we're eternal, spiritual beings made of pure consciousness and energy? To not be in touch with this component of ourselves is to not be in touch with an aspect of ourselves that is divinely given.

Intuition

Many of us utilize our psychic abilities in our daily lives without realizing we're doing so. One of the most common occurrences is knowing that the phone is about to ring just before it does or hearing from an old friend within a short time of thinking about that person. Perhaps you've been saved from tragedy when something told you to turn right instead of left or to not do something you were about to do. Maybe you were walking down the street and got a bad feeling about someone who was approaching you, so you moved out of the way.

These are all examples of intuition at work. The types of messages and information that come to us through our sixth sense are not communications from angels or spirit guides. They merely show that you're attuned to the energy and vibrations around you. They're part of our makeup as living beings.

An intuitive hunch is often referred to as a gut feeling. This is closer to the truth than you might imagine, because the chakra associated with

6 http://en.wikipedia.org/wiki/Extra-sensory_perception

intuition is located in our gut or stomach area. This, the third chakra, or solar plexus chakra, is also called the second brain. It's the seat of knowing.

Any time you know something in your heart or in your gut, you're listening to your sixth sense. You may hold certain beliefs that others question, asking you, "How do you know that? Where's your proof?" You shake your head and say, "I just know." That's intuition. It sometimes requires great faith on our part to rely on this inner guidance, but when we don't pay attention, we often come to regret it.

In December of 2003, the area of northern New Jersey where I live had a severe blizzard. Being the workaholic that I am, I wasn't about to sit at home and do nothing. The morning after the storm I made my way to the angel gift shop I owned. I had a long list of to-do's, including taking a bunch of cardboard to be recycled. This was obviously something that could have waited until the roads were clear, but all I could think about was scratching one more job off my list.

As I rushed about the shop gathering up boxes, I clearly heard a voice in my head telling me, "Don't do that today." My intuition told me to leave the boxes alone, but did I listen? Of course not. As I carried the boxes to the car, my legs slipped right out from under me, and down I went onto the hard pavement. I broke my arm and shoulder so badly that I had to be taken to the hospital by ambulance. The artificial joint that replaced the shattered bones is a daily reminder to me of the importance of listening to that inner voice.

Make every effort to listen to your intuition throughout the day. Pay attention to the subtle messages you receive. It's as simple as listening to your feelings, thoughts, and hunches, but far too few people take the time to quiet their minds. They let the rampant thoughts rushing around drown out everything.

Once you begin to tune in to your inner sensors, you can use this source of information in all aspects of your life, whether for business decisions, questions about your personal life, or the many simple decisions we make from moment to moment. For example, you feel that your Aunt Mary needs you, so you call her.

Learn to ask yourself if the choice you're about to make is the best course of action: Should you go on that trip, even though you have a bad feeling about it? Your intuition will be right far more often than your rational mind.

As you begin to work with and allow your intuition to guide you, it will become a tremendous asset in your mediumship. It can help you to determine if you're interpreting the information you're receiving in the correct manner. For example, let's say you perceive a spirit communicator that comes to you as a father. At that point you could ask yourself if this information feels correct to you. If you're intuition tells you that this is not a father, but a grandfather, you can alter your message.

Mediumship is not an exact science. Messages from the other side are often open to interpretation. You may sense that a spirit crossed to the other side from a heart attack, but your gut instinct tells you that's not correct. In that case, you can silently ask for more information. Do not underestimate the power of your sixth sense. It will aid in your journey through life and particularly in your mediumship as you grow.

Telepathy

As a Spiritualist and a medium, I believe that the mind continues after death and that communication between our minds and the minds of those who have crossed over is a reality. Because we are eternal spirits, it stands to reason that communication is possible between the minds of those of us still in physical form as well. Telepathy is the word that describes the unseen communication between individuals. It has also been referred to as *thought transference* and can involve directing our thoughts to a particular person.

Thoughts are energy with their own vibration. Mediums are particularly attuned to the energy of thoughts, but certain individuals who have not developed their mediumship can also be highly telepathic. Think about married couples who are so attuned to each other's thoughts that don't need to talk to know what their partner wants. The same holds true for twins, like my two nieces, and mothers and their children who can have a very strong mind-to-mind relationship. Many mothers tell me about knowing what their child is thinking or doing, even when they're miles apart.

I use telepathy during my readings. When an individual comes to me for a private session, I try to determine what's on the person's mind by focusing on their thoughts. I ask myself why they are seeking me out, particularly if they're not looking for a mediumistic reading and want me to look at the course of coming events in their lives. After years of practice, I can easily read the "signs" or subtle energy that we all emanate.

Learning how to incorporate your psychic abilities into your life is not difficult, but it does take awareness, time and practice. The awareness part of the equation relates to learning to be conscious of your sixth sense and tuning in to the hunches and gut feelings your intuition sends your way every moment of the day. As for the time and practice, I'm going to share with you now an exercise designed specifically to increase your telepathic ability:

Exercise 4.1
-   Find a partner who is willing to work with you. Preferably, you'll find someone who wants to improve their telepathic ability along with you, but if the thought transference is only one way, with you being the receiver, that's okay, too.
-   Sit directly across from your partner. Sit close to each other, but not touching.
-   Decide who will be the sender and who will be the receiver.
-   Both receiver and sender close their eyes.
-   The sender concentrates on a number from one to ten. She holds that number in her mind and makes a conscious effort to send the number across to the recipient.
-   The receiver states aloud the first thought or feeling she has without analyzing.
-   The sender informs the receiver if she was correct or not, then moves on to another number from one to ten.

Note: The sender should not repeat a number once it has been used in a single session. The goal is to quiet the rational mind and let the feeling mind sense or receive the impression. Repeating numbers causes the rational mind to try and guess. This is not guess-work. It is attunement to thought-energy, which does not occur at the level of the rational mind.

-   Once you have worked with numbers for several minutes, continue in the same method, only now the sender will transmit thoughts of

shapes. Use only a handful of agreed-upon shapes, such as a heart, a star, a square, a circle, and a triangle.
- When finished with shapes, move on to basic colors. Again, use only a handful of agreed-upon colors such as red, blue, green, orange, yellow, and purple.
- When finished with numbers, shapes, and colors, switch roles if desired, with the sender now being the receiver.

Any amount of effort you put into this exercise will help, but I recommend that you practice at least once a week for half an hour. Naturally, the more often you work on these skills, the better the results. As time goes on, you will see improvement in your ability to discern your partner's thoughts. Feel free to make things a little harder at that point. Increase the range of items you're working with.

Don't get discouraged if you have no trouble stating the right shape or color, but can't get the numbers correct. I've discovered that most people are better at one category than another. No matter what your results, don't give up if you're not initially successful. I can't state that strongly enough. Developing your skill takes practice. You can't expect to see improvement unless you work at it.

William James, the American psychologist and philosopher, said, "We are making use of only a small part of our possible mental and physical resources."[7] Those of us who develop our sixth sense and our telepathy work to counteract that statement. To not use all of our senses in our lives, including our sixth sense, is to not live fully. Use all of the gifts that God has given you, and live your life to the fullest.

---

7 http://faculty.washington.edu/chudler/tenper.html

PART II

TOOLS OF DEVELOPMENT

Chapter 5
Meditation

Following the path of mediumship will undoubtedly change your life, so as we begin this section of the book dealing with methods of development, it's important to stop and take a moment to ask a very important question: Do you really know *yourself*?

I'm not talking about the part of you that identifies with the external you: your profession, how you look, or your role within your family. Those are all ego identities that change over time. I'm talking about the part of you that never changes … the part of you that is eternal. Call it your soul, your spirit, your Self … whatever you call it, the ego is pretty good at shouting so loudly that you may never hear that "still, small voice" inside of you until you quiet all the external noise.

If you don't really know your interior self, don't feel bad. You're not alone. There are plenty of people who have no interior life. They're totally consumed with the physical, material world. They may be considered successful by society's standards. They may appear happy and content, and that's fine. I don't want to lessen anyone's achievements, but without accessing the self, any true happiness or success is only temporary.

A focus on the development of your interior world should form the basis of your spiritual life. One of the best ways to develop your interior world is through meditation. It's hugely important for the evolution of your soul and for the development of your mediumship. In my mind, you can't separate the two. Yes, there are mediums who will say differently, but to me, there's a huge spiritual component to communicating with the unseen world.

The only way to get to know your true self is through the silence of your inner world. Nuns, monks, and other religious people know the value of silence. When I lived in a convent, I used to spend full days in quiet prayer and contemplation. Some people go off into caves in the Himalayas to meet themselves. But you don't have to go halfway around the world or join a convent to make your own acquaintance. The silence is always there, even on a busy train in downtown Manhattan. You just need to learn how to find it.

Inside yourself is where true, lasting peace is found, and that peace can be accessed in the silence of meditation. For most people, their minds are never still from the moment they awaken in the morning until they drift off to sleep each night. They flit from one thought to the next in constant succession, always thinking, plotting, dwelling on the past, or worrying about the future. It's no wonder so many people are over-stressed.

Think of your mind as a pond. Your thoughts lie at the surface, often whipping the water into tiny whitecaps. Thankfully, the disturbances lessen the deeper you go, until you get to the bottom of the pond where the water is still and peaceful. Meditation allows you to sink down into the deep recesses of your mind and enjoy your natural state—the infinite peacefulness of your very being.

I first learned to meditate at a beautiful retreat center where I went with a group of friends. There I was free to wander the secluded grounds to my heart's content. I was pretty new to the whole concept of quiet reflection. I'd never bothered to try and still my restless mind. Instead, I carried around a whole headfull of destructive thoughts and images from my childhood, giving them free rein to run around inside my brain. Their constant negative chatter formed the very foundation of my belief system.

Growing up, I hadn't gone to church much, but I was no stranger to prayer. I'd spent a lifetime pleading for God to help me. Sitting under the thick canopy of trees at that retreat center, I did my best to quiet the chatter in my mind. It was a whole new concept for me—just sitting there with no other purpose than to listen, but I came to love that time spent in silence. Today, I can't imagine getting through the day without prayer and meditation. It's even more important to me than my daily trip to Starbucks, and that's saying a lot!

Mediumship is a mental activity. In our daily lives, we spend the vast majority of our days operating in a physical environment, using our five senses to interpret our surroundings and sensations. The messages from the spirit world, however, don't enter our mind through our physical eyes, ears, nose, mouth, and skin. They come through the counterparts of those senses in our spirit (or ethereal) body.

The key to communicating with the spirit world is being able to quiet the normal, everyday chatter of your conscious mind and becoming receptive to the far more subtle thoughts, images, and feelings that come from those in spirit. The best way to do that is to meditate on a regular basis. But first, before we get into the ins and outs of meditation, make no mistake: when you make that link with the spirit world, your mind is *not* in a meditative state; it's in an accelerated state—attuned to the much higher mental vibrations of the spirit world. It's almost hypersensitivity, but there's a point of stillness there as well.

That may seem contradictory, but it's not. When your mind is hypersensitive yet still, you've gotten your conscious mind out of the picture and brought your receptive mind to the forefront. You want your mind to become like a mirror onto which the spirit world can reflect their thoughts and images. The great British spiritual healer Harry Edwards called this the "mirror of your mind." You want to clear that mirror so the spirit world can put something there for you to perceive. To do that, you have to train the receptive mind to be receptive and the thinking, rational mind to step quietly into the background. Sitting in the silence of meditation is the most effective way to do that.

There are many forms of meditation. The various methods span the religious traditions from Zen and Tibetan Buddhism, to Taoism, Hinduism, Islam, Judaism, and Christianity. While they may differ in subtlety, all share certain similarities. Dr. David Fontana, a British meditation teacher and psychologist has written several excellent books on the subject. He advocates approaching meditation without preconceived ideas of what you want to happen. You should keep an open mind and not set any goals for your sessions.[8]

Enjoy meditation for meditation's sake, but developing inner stillness is key. For me, it wouldn't matter if I were on a busy train in New York City if I needed to center myself, but to get the true benefits of meditation, the quiet piece is critical. Find a place where you can have half an hour of peace. If that's impossible in your home, go to a park or even a church

8 Fontana, David. *Learn to Meditate*, Chronicle Books LLC, London, 1999. p.15.

before or after services. Ideally, you should sit in a comfortable chair where you have plenty of privacy and no distractions. For this, you may have to get out of bed early or stay up after the kids have gone to sleep.

Sit comfortably with your feet flat on the floor. Place your hands on your thighs. It doesn't matter if they're facing up or down. Do whatever is most comfortable for you. Begin with a few long, slow, deep breaths. As you do so, consciously relax all of the muscles in your body to the best of your ability. Start with the top of your head and work your way down through your face to your shoulders and on through your torso and your arms and legs to your fingers and toes. Release the tension from every muscle and joint you encounter along the way.

Once your body is relaxed, turn your focus even more to your breathing. Mentally watch and listen to each inhalation and exhalation. This act will make it easier to quiet your mind. Don't worry if thoughts intrude into the silence. The biggest mistake beginning meditators make is thinking that they have to block out all thoughts from their mind. This is a nearly impossible task and only causes mental tension—the exact opposite state from the one you want to achieve.

Whenever thoughts, worries, or anxieties distract you from being present to meditation, don't resist them. Simply allow them to drift away as you refocus on your breathing. You may find it helpful to silently repeat a word or phrase that is spiritually significant to you, such as *love* ... or *peace* ...

With time and practice, you'll be able to slow down your brain waves and enter into an altered state of consciousness. I'll discuss different types of brain waves as they relate to consciousness later in the book. For now, simply know that the light altered state which you can achieve through normal meditation allows your mind to be more receptive to the spirit world. It is not a trance state. You are still aware of your surroundings. If someone talks or something makes a noise, you'll hear these things, but you'll remain in this deep state of relaxation until you deliberately bring yourself out of it.

If you're serious about becoming the best medium you can be, you need to make a sincere commitment to regular periods of meditation. If you can give it a lot of time, that's great. There have been times in my life when I had the luxury of giving an hour a day, but sometimes I can only give 5-10 minutes. That's okay, too. It's the commitment that counts.

I want to warn you that if you're new to meditation, don't expect instant changes. Don't sit there expecting to immediately see blinding lights or experience ecstatic revelations. While those kind of spiritual experiences are always possible in meditation, the benefits from meditation are more subtle. You're guaranteed to feel more relaxed and at peace after every session, but the long-term benefits of meditation—the increased sensitivity and receptivity to the spirit world—are cumulative and develop with continued practice. Enjoy each session knowing that by training your mind to be still, you'll be far more aware of that still small voice making its presence known, even in the midst of chaos.

Only in silence can you learn to attune yourself to the power that is within and around you. Only in silence can you become more receptive to the wisdom and inspiration, the truth and the knowledge that is available to those willing to access it. Make a commitment to retreat regularly into the silence of your being. Leave the physical world behind and tune in to the subtle, delicate vibrations of the spirit life around you. It is there, in the peace and quiet, that you learn to harmonize with the minds of the spirit world who are so anxious to have a conduit through which they can reach our world.

There comes a time when the spirit world itself begins to train its instrument. That can only take place if you put time into the silence. Make meditation a habit, for your sake and theirs. Take time to sit in the stillness- bask in the power of the spirit's influence and attune your receptive self to the spirit's presence.

Chapter 6
Auras and Color Analysis

Think back to a time when you walked into a room where moments earlier two people had been arguing. How did the room feel? Were you able to sense the lingering tension and anger? If so, you had tuned in to the auric energy the couple left behind. Now imagine that you've arranged to meet the same couple for dinner later that evening. You walk into the restaurant and sit down across from them. Even though they both greet you pleasantly and smile, it's immediately obvious that they still haven't settled their differences. Why? Because their energy field is radiating their emotional state at you like a huge electrical transformer. Others around you may not be able to sense their mood, but you can. Why? Because you're reading their aura and the residue energy.

The aura is the electro-magnetic energy field that permeates physical objects and radiates outward from them. Because everything is made of energy and vibration, everything has an aura. The auras of living beings are a manifestation of the subtle life force within the body.

We all have a personal electromagnetic field around us that reflects our unique vibration. The aura expands and shrinks with the force of the energy. Highly spiritual people have an expanded aura that seems to fill a room when they enter. My favorite saint, St. Theresa, is said to have had this effect.

There are people who are born with the ability to see the aura without any training. You may learn to develop this ability, but don't get discouraged if, after much trying, you can't look at a person and see their auric field. Clairvoyance isn't the only way to tune into spirit vibrations. It's only one of several methods at a medium's disposal. Using clairsentience, you can learn to sense a person's aura, whether they're in spirit or still in physical form. It's all about reading subtle energy.

Here's a quick exercise to show you what the human energy field looks like. A more in-depth exercise follows:

Exercise 6.1

Stand or sit in a lighted room in front of a dark background, such as a black curtain, a dark piece of furniture, or perhaps a few feet away from a darkened television screen. Hold your arms up with elbows at chest height and the palms of both hands facing your body about a foot and a half away from your face. Both thumbs should point up and the fingers of your right hand should be no more than one-half to one inch away from the fingers of the left hand, directly in front of your eyes. Keep your fingers loosely apart.

Stare at the empty space between all of your fingers and between the tips of the fingers of your left and right hands. Continue to stare, but let your eyes go out of focus and relax your mind. You should soon see a subtle glow that follows the outline of your fingers. Note the glow and stay with it. Soon you should see the energy radiating from your finger tips, flowing like tendrils of wispy white smoke and joining the energy from the opposite fingers of each hand.

That wispy, smoke-like glow is your energy field. Once you're able to see the glow of your aura around your fingers, you're ready to try to move on to seeing it on a larger scale.

Exercise 6.2

Stand in front of a large mirror in a softly lighted room. The wall behind you should be a solid, light color such as beige or white. (Bathrooms work well for this exercise). Keeping in mind that it's more difficult to see the aura through clothing, focus on the area from your neck up. Choose one spot to look at, such as the middle of your forehead. Just as in exercise 5.1, keep your eyes on this spot, but allow them to go out of focus. With your peripheral vision, you should be able to see a subtle glow around the outline of your head and neck. If the glow goes in and out, work on maintaining just the right level of non-focus so that you remain attuned to this subtle energy. Once you become skilled at seeing your own aura, you can try the same experiment on others under various conditions.

When I give a reading, I imagine that I'm putting on the overcoat of the person I'm trying to paint back to life. As I mentally slip their coat over my shoulders, I tune into the energy that now surrounds me. The auric field can be read on four distinct levels, each of which gives us insight into a person or spirit's character or condition:

Emotional: Reading a person's aura on an emotional level will tell you things such as if the person cries at the drop of a hat or is cool and aloof. You could sense if you're dealing with someone who is compassionate or callous, upbeat or down in the dumps. I had a man come into my office years ago whose aura at the emotional level immediately put me on alert. The man wasn't unkempt or disheveled, but I could tell from assessing his energy that he was emotionally unstable. This was more than the gut instinct or intuition we talked about earlier. I was attuned to the negative energy he was projecting. I found out later that the man was a stalker. I have to admit that I wasn't surprised. To me, his emotional aura was like a red flag.

Mental: Be careful not to confuse a person's emotional energy with their mental energy. The man in the previous example may have had mental problems, but I was reading his emotional energy. In reading a person's aura on a mental level, you're looking more at the way their mind works. Are they good at numbers? Are they quick and sharp or easily confused? Perhaps they're obsessive-compulsive. You can sense all of this and more when you focus on the mental energy field.

Physical: A healthy body will radiate a completely different energy from one that's sick. Disease and sickness show up in the aura just as clearly as physical vibrancy. I once had a client come to me for a reading and I sensed immediately from her aura that something bad was going on at a physical level. I'm not trained in medicine and I hate to diagnose illness, but I felt an obligation to tell the woman what I felt. I specifically sensed that the metal levels in her body were way out of balance, and I advised her to see a doctor right away. Luckily, she listened to me and went for testing. Her doctor identified a physical problem that needed immediate attention. In obvious cases, even an untrained person can tell if a person isn't well just by their appearance. A medium who is trained in reading auras can use this gift to detect more subtle physical issues that aren't readily visible.

Spiritual: Jesus, various saints, and angels are often depicted in paintings with a glowing halo around their head. This is a not-so subtle representation of the subtle aura of highly spiritual beings. People who live their lives attuned to spirit radiate a type of energy that others feel simply by being in their presence. The higher vibrating aura of a spiritual person feels completely different to a medium than that of a person who is mired in materialism.

The aura is made up of electro-magnetic energy. Color is also made up of electro-magnetic energy vibrating at different frequencies or wavelengths along a spectrum which our physical eyes can perceive. For those of us who can see auras, we usually detect different colors within the energy field. As the frequency or wavelength of a person's energy changes, so does the color.

We can use these changes in color to provide us information about people. For example, let's say that I see a beautiful pink color surrounding one of my clients. That tells me the person is feeling very loving at the moment. However, the color may turn to red if they become angry.

Different colors may mean different things to different people, but each has significance on the four levels discussed earlier. I look around the head to detect mental characteristics and at the top of the head for spiritual characteristics. Emotional characteristics or issues would show up around the heart, and physical issues could surround the entire body or be in a specific problem area.

Once again, keep in mind that you don't have to be clairvoyant to use color. Because color is a result of variations in energy, you can learn to sense them without seeing them so that colors have the same meaning to you as they would to a clairvoyant on each of the four levels. The following is a list of the generally accepted meanings for various colors:

Red. On the emotional level, I associate red with passion, liveliness, anger, or frustration. It's a powerful color, so on a mental level I associate it with high energy or self-confidence. If you see a red aura or sense a red feeling around a person, it could also mean that on a spiritual level they are highly materialistic and are more interested in the physical world than the spiritual. People with a red feel to them are likely to be skeptical about things they can't see, hear, touch, or taste. On a physical level, the color red could indicate strength or sensuality.

Orange. Being so close in vibration to red, orange is another powerful color. In fact, it can actually indicate that the person has a lot of personal power, or perhaps the desire or ability to control other people. Physically, orange indicates someone who is energetic and who may like to push the limits and challenge themselves. Orange indicates pride as well as cunning and a need for excitement.

Yellow. If you run across a person who is bright and cheery, free-spirited and almost childlike in their personality, their aura is likely yellow. The color also indicates a person with a great sense of humor who loves to laugh. I associate yellow with the mind and the intellect, although a person with a yellow aura would tend to want to work at something creative if they had to work at all.

Green. Most healers have green in their aura. The color is also associated with individualism, adaptability, and prosperity. Mentally, green indicates a strong intellect in a person who can process ideas and information quickly. A person with green in their aura may be highly competitive and may be drawn to money and business. Green also indicates harmony, sympathy, balance, and peace.

Blue. Don't fall into the trap of thinking that a blue aura means a person is "blue" in the sense of being "down in the dumps." If you see or sense blue around a person, you're likely dealing with someone who is balanced, inspirational, and even noble. Their blue aura shows that they are loving and nurturing and possibly religious. A darker shade of blue such as indigo would indicate that the person may have natural psychic and intuitive abilities.

Purple. On a spiritual level, you can't get much better than purple or violet. This color indicates wisdom, self-mastery, and high spiritual attainment. People with purple auras have a higher love of humanity than most and a strongly developed sense of intuition.

Pink. Like blue, to me pink indicates that a person is loving and gentle. It's the emotional color of love and happiness.

White. Like purple, I associate white with someone who is pure and spiritual.

Gray. Gray is one of those colors that has a universal feel to it, and it's never positive. Gray is associated with dark thoughts and possibly a dark personality. I had a client come to my office whose aura was so gray that I knew he was thinking of killing himself. Yes, I could sense his depression on a psychic level, but his gray aura convinced me to put him in touch with a counselor I trusted.

I recommend that you commit these meanings to memory. As time goes on and you develop the ability to read auras—either clairvoyantly or with clairsentience--knowing what the various colors mean will help you immeasurably. You can begin by studying the people you interact with daily. Look at the colors they choose to wear or the colors they surround themselves with in their homes. From there, move on to trying to read the colors in their auric field. Do the same thing when you're in a café with strangers sitting nearby or walking down the street. Try to sense the colors associated with them on each of the four levels.

Once again, you don't have to be able to see colors to "read" them. Studies with blind people have shown that even people without physical sight can sense the colors of objects by tuning into the different energy each color emits. The following exercise is designed to help you increase your attunement to the subtle variations in the vibrations of different colors.

Exercise 6.3

Gather some tissue paper or ribbons of different colors. Make sure that whatever you choose, each piece is made of the same material so that you can't differentiate between them based on texture. If working with a partner, close your eyes and have your partner drape one of the ribbons or pieces of tissue paper on you. Try to sense the color. If working alone, mix up the ribbons with your eyes closed, choose one at a time to hold and try to sense its color.

As a student of mediumship who wants to strengthen your abilities, you need to develop a strong foundation of general information you can build upon. By the time you finish reading this book, you'll have a variety of tools available to you in your mediumship toolbox. Because the aura can reveal details you might not get through other methods, an understanding of the human energy field and colors is one of the basic tools for accessing information.

After you become adept at reading the colors of physical beings, it's simply a matter of transferring this skill to the spirit world to get valuable evidence about what the entity was like on each of the four levels. When you can describe a spirit to your client emotionally, mentally, physically, and spiritually based on clues from the energy and colors you sense in them, you're building a strong body of evidence that you are, indeed, communicating with their loved ones.

Chapter 7

Chakras

We are vibrating, energetic beings. Physics has proven that everything in creation constantly vibrates back and forth between matter and energy, or physical and etheric. Vital life force flows throughout every cell in our bodies, maintaining our health and our physical body's very existence.

As you learned in the last chapter, the aura is the personal electromagnetic field around each of us that reflects our unique vibration. Chinese medical practitioners have worked with human energy, or "chi" for thousands of years. The western world is much slower to pay attention to the importance of energy flow in our bodies, but Spiritualists are ahead of the curve. We've known since the beginning of the modern movement that we are primarily spiritual beings made of vibrating energy and we use this knowledge in healing and in working with the spirit world.

An important component of the body's energy system are the concentrated centers of energy in the head, neck, and lined up along the spine known as *chakras*. This concentration of energy is now measurable with scientific instruments, but Hindu yogis throughout the ages have been able to directly perceive each of the seven energy centers in altered states of consciousness. The word "chakra" (pronounced *SHAH-krah*) comes from the Sanskrit language and means "wheel." There are seven major chakras which are part of the etheric body where the life energy gathers and circulates like an eddy or whirlpool. They have been compared to etheric transformers, taking the energy that is all around us and transforming it into the correct frequency we need for different life functions.

Diagrams of the chakras within the body show them as distinct orbs, but it's important to realize that each chakra is connected by a river of energy flowing within the spinal column. The level of energy concentrated at each chakra is always changing. The energy whirlpools can be large and pulsating, or there could be a blockage which could result in sluggishness or disease in the physical body. The ideal state is for the flow to be unimpeded in both directions and for all seven chakras to be vibrant and equal in size, or balanced.

The chakras belong to our spirit bodies, but knowing that our spirit body is a mirror image of our physical bodies, it's interesting to note that these energy centers are co-located with actual physical concentrations of nerve ganglia throughout the body. Each chakra is also located near and associated with vital organs and glands whose health and functioning is directly affected by the energy in the chakra.

Chakras have a tremendous influence on our physical health, but there is an equally important emotional and mental aspect associated with them. Because every thought and emotion has its own vibration, each chakra corresponds to a particular facet along the entire spectrum of human experience. While the vibrancy of the chakras can affect our physical energy level, emotions, and health, it works both ways. We can directly influence the chakras with our thoughts, our emotions, our diet, our level of physical activity, and even our breath.

The chakras are referred to either by number (the first through the seventh, always starting with the chakra closest to the earth) or by physical location. The frequency of the energy in each chakra increases from the first through the seventh chakra, with the crown chakra having the highest, most refined energy. Each chakra is also associated with a specific color which can be perceived by those able to see the aura.

The spirit world uses these energy centers to send specific types of information. It's possible to shift your consciousness from awareness of the physical body to an awareness of more subtle spirit vibrations by tuning into or focusing on each of the seven chakras. From this awareness you can tap into impressions from the other side which you might otherwise not be conscious of.

The following is a review of each chakra's role and the types of information you can tune into with specific energy centers to help you in your mediumship:

1. The base (or root) chakra

This energy center is located at the base of the spine near the coccyx. Because it's the lowest chakra, closest to the earth, this center has the most basic energy. The root chakra is involved with our need for the basic necessities of life, such as food and shelter. The energy from the base chakra supplies our body with vitality and supports our will to live. An unbalanced first chakra would cause a person to be anxious and afraid. By meditating and focusing on this chakra, we can help ourselves to feel more grounded, secure, and physically powerful.

The root chakra is associated with the color red, which we learned in the last chapter can indicate passion, anger, power, or even frustration—all very earthly attributes.

2. The navel chakra

The second chakra, as its alternate name implies, is located in the abdomen just beneath the navel. Because it lies within the area of the sexual organs, it is associated with reproduction, sexuality, relationships, and physical enjoyment. When energy flows freely through the second chakra, we feel healthy pleasure. An unbalanced navel chakra can lead to emotional problems such as guilt or over attachment. The second chakra is associated with the color orange.

3. The solar plexus chakra

The point just below the center of the chest at the level of the diaphragm is the solar plexus, also called the third chakra. It is known as the power center because through it we manifest our will. By focusing your awareness on this area, you can energize the third chakra, resulting in better digestion, less fatigue, as well as acceptance of yourself and others.

A vibrant third chakra results in joy, laughter, and a sense of purpose. If the third chakra is in need of healing, a person could feel fear or anger, and because this chakra is the center of willpower, they may have an abundance of aggression. By learning to balance this energy center, we can bring our physical and emotional state into moderation instead of allowing the two to vacillate between extremes. The third chakra is associated with the color yellow.

In older days, mediums called the third chakra the second brain. Today we know it more as the seat of clairsentience. The solar plexus chakra is the source of those gut feelings we talked about earlier and is a valuable tool for mediumship. If you're giving a reading and your gut says "something isn't right with that information," you can come up with a different way of interpreting what you're getting from the other side. That shift could be the difference between giving an outstanding message and a mediocre one. If you're giving a public demonstration and your gut says you're not with the right recipient, try to find the intended recipient of your message.

4. The heart chakra

As its name implies, this energy center is located in the area of the heart. As you might guess, it's the seat of the primary emotional energy of the universe: love. It is also the seat of understanding, and being situated halfway between the first and seventh chakras, it acts to balance the energy below with the energy above. A vibrant heart chakra leads to greater confidence and compassion. The energy flow in a person's heart chakra may need healing due to some emotional hurt in the past, resulting in feelings of loss, grief, or sadness. Green is the color associated with the heart chakra.

I feel that the heart chakra hasn't been developed enough in mediumship. The thinking mind is rational, but the heart is all feeling, which is the way a medium should be perceiving spirit messages: feeling, not thinking. Focusing on this area during a reading or demonstration can be a great help to a medium in sensing the relationship of the discarnate spirit to the sitter they are working with. There's often an actual physical response when you connect with a spirit through the heart chakra. I can tell from the feeling in my chest how much people cared for one another. If I'm talking to a spirit communicator and my heart just melts, I'm able to tell the sitter, "This guy really adored you!"

5. The throat chakra

The fifth chakra, located in the throat near the thyroid gland, is the center of communication, which includes talking as well as listening. It's the closest power center to the area between the two ears, so for this reason, the throat chakra is associated with clairaudience. It's also associated with creativity and serves as the bridge between thinking and feeling. We can use the energy from this area to interpret spiritual insights. A fifth chakra with free-flowing energy helps us to feel clear-minded and express ourselves freely. A fifth chakra that needs healing leads to fear of expression. Light blue is the color associated with the throat chakra.

6. The third eye (or brow) chakra

If clairsentience is associated with the solar plexus chakra and clairaudience with the throat chakra, it should be obvious that clairvoyance goes hand in hand with the third eye chakra. By focusing on this area while connecting with the spirit world, you may find that you're able to perceive images more clearly.

This power center is located in the center of the skull at the brow level between the two physical eyes and is associated with self-awareness, higher consciousness, insight, and a sense of "knowing" when flowing freely. Poor vision, bad dreams, and headaches can all be symptoms of poorly flowing energy in the sixth chakra. The brow chakra is associated with the color indigo, or dark blue.

7. The crown chakra

Unlike all of the other chakras, the seventh chakra is located outside of the physical body, at the top of the skull. It is the seat of spirituality, and as such, has the highest, most refined vibration of all of the chakras. It is associated with the color violet, a color which always indicates spirituality to those who can read auras. It's responsible for thinking and awareness. A balanced crown chakra results in spiritual balance and a feeling of connection with God. Poor energy flow in the seventh chakra can lead to skepticism, confusion, and apathy.

The following exercise will help you to familiarize yourself with your personal power centers. This is an excellent meditation to do when you're out of balance and need to center yourself.

Exercise 7.1. Chakra Meditation

Find a place where you won't be disturbed for at least half an hour. Sit comfortably with your feet flat on the floor, hands in your lap, and eyes closed. Inhale and exhale slowly and deeply, relaxing all parts of your body as you would for a normal meditation. When thoroughly relaxed and your mind is as still as possible, begin the following visualization:

Imagine a closed lotus flower at the top of your head where the crown chakra is located. Focus on the lotus and picture its leaves opening and blooming. Once you have this image firmly in your mind, feel a beautiful vine running down from the crown chakra to the third eye or brow chakra. Picture a closed lotus here as well. Focus the energy with your mind and see this new lotus slowly, slowly opening.

Now imagine the vine running down to the throat chakra and picture a lotus at this energy center. Focus the energy so the lotus opens just as the others did, then follow the vine down to the heart chakra. Continue in this way, slowly and deliberately. Picture the vine running to each of the remaining energy centers (solar plexus, navel, and root/base chakras) with a closed lotus at each one. Take your time and open the flowers by concentrating the energy with your mind.

When you've finished with the root chakra, continue extending the vine all the way through your body until it connects you to the earth. Focus on your breathing and the balance that you've created. After a few minutes release the focus and begin to see the lotuses close one by one from the root chakra to the crown chakra. Feel your feet grounded to the earth and shift your consciousness back to the space you're in.

How did that feel? At the very least you should feel calm and relaxed when finished the meditation. Practicing this exercise over the long term will improve your health and increase your vitality. It will also get you used to focusing on the individual energy centers. For mediums, focusing your awareness on the chakras while giving a reading helps by turning you away from your physical senses and tuning you in to your interior world.

As I mentioned earlier, these are the areas through which you receive the subtle messages from spirit. You can heighten your sensitivity to these areas by practicing the type of mediumship associated with each particular chakra while focusing on the associated energy center (clairvoyance with the brow chakra, clairaudience with the throat chakra, and clairsentience with the heart chakra and the solar plexus chakra). The following exercise should get you started:

Exercise 7.2. Sit quietly and take a few deep breaths. Focus your attention on the brow chakra and picture an old man walking down the street. Now move your attention to your throat chakra and hear the sound of church bells ringing in the distance. Focus on your heart chakra and feel the emotion of a mother and child reunited after a long separation. Now jump back up to the throat chakra and hear the sound of really hard rain on a metal roof. Move down to the solar plexus chakra and feel what you would experience if you saw a dangerous-looking man walking down the street toward you.

You get the idea. You can take this kind of practice as far as your imagination allows. The spirit people send you the same kind of split-second images, sounds, and sensations as you experience when doing this exercise. They give you quick impressions, and it's your job as a medium to sense them and pass them along. Focusing on the chakras can only help to strengthen the impressions you receive.

I have to admit that I don't consciously think about the chakras when I'm working. The images have become such a part of me that I just tune in to them no matter where they're coming from in my body. Your goal should be to get to the same point, but for now you should be aware of the presence of these power centers in your body and the role they play in helping you to receive information. A knowledge of chakras becomes part of your tool box and helps you to be the best medium you can be.

Chapter 8

Psychometry

Did you ever watch the Johnny Carson show? You may be too young to have seen his late night program, but I'll never forget when he used to do his routine as the psychic, Carnac the Magnificent. He'd come out on stage in a huge red turban and a flowing black cape. In his hand he held a stack of "hermetically sealed" envelopes.

One by one he would place an envelope against his forehead and divine the answer to a question that was supposedly written inside. His sidekick, Ed McMahon, would egg Johnny on, and the resulting jokes were *bad*. I mean really corny, like the time when Carnac held an envelope against his forehead, thought for a moment, then said, "Sis boom bah." Ed McMahon repeated "Sis boom bah," then Carnac ripped open the envelope and read, "Describe the sound that's made when a sheep explodes."

Sorry about that. I couldn't help myself. Mediumship may be sacred work, but as I learned from my British friends, you gotta have some fun with it, too.

Johnny Carson may have been joking around on his show, but what he was doing with the envelopes is actually pretty close to an exercise I use in my classes when I teach about psychometry. All joking aside, a knowledge of psychometry and practical experience in applying that knowledge can greatly improve your attunement to the spirit world.

Psychometry is the ability to read the residual energy left behind with physical objects. All living things vibrate with life force. Inanimate objects also have a vibration, but it's far more subtle than that of plants, animals, and people. The vibration is caused by the movement of the electrons within the atoms. This energy is part of what a medium senses whey they touch an object, but they also sense the residual energy from other things that have come in contact with that object over time.

As an example, think about a ring that's been handed down from generation to generation. That piece of jewelry is imprinted with the unique vibrations of the person who created it as well as the vibrations of everyone who wore it over the years. A person trained in psychometry can hold the ring and tap into its past by sensing each unique vibration held within its atoms.

Psychometry helps you to look past just what you see with your physical eyes and become aware of the actual history of objects. I clearly remember the day that one of my students brought an arrowhead to class. The moment I picked up that pointy, weathered stone I saw a horrible massacre before my eyes. I heard explosions, sensed pure hatred, and felt the shock of violent death. I saw large red rock formations and was overwhelmed with a feeling of great sadness—all from one little arrowhead.

The vibration and the resulting information you can gain from objects changes drastically from article to article. Imagine the things you could sense walking around an antique store. It would be like a trip back in time. Most people pass through life—not just antique stores—completely unaware of the vast amount of information available to all of us through our extra sensory perception.

Places can be filled with residual energy just like objects can. The former concentration camp at Auschwitz is a prime example of a place that oozes negative energy, just like battlefields such as Normandy or Gettysburg. Many people have the mistaken idea that ghosts haunt such places, because they can sense the vibrations of people who lost their lives there or maybe even hear the names of the dead. Trust me, the spirit people aren't hanging around such negative places. What visitors feel is the high amount of residual energy left behind due to the intensity of the events that happened there.

Psychometry can be highly valuable in working with missing persons cases. When I do that kind of work, I always ask for an article of clothing that the missing individual has worn, preferably unwashed. The moment I touch the person's belongings, I'm flooded with information about them: images, words, and thoughts that show me where they might be or what might have happened to them. That first impression is usually right, so I pass along everything I get.

Psychometry is helpful for locating missing persons, but I don't think a medium should need to hold anything during a reading or demonstration. People who come to me often have a certain level of skepticism. My job is to give them overwhelming evidence that their loved ones are around. I don't want to give anyone a reason to think I had some kind of special help or that something they handed me gave me any hints. You don't need crutches. At some point you have to fly on your own merits.

Having said that, psychometry is a valuable tool for developing your mediumship. In my psychic development classes, I deliberately work with psychometry to increase my students' ability to read subtle energy. I pass around sealed envelopes containing pictures of people and places. I ask the class to write down the images they get from holding the envelopes. Later, they share with the group what they sensed, saw, or heard. Even without holding the envelopes to their foreheads, they usually find they're much more accurate than Carnac the Magnificent.

Here's an exercise you can try with a friend:

Exercise 8.1

Have your partner place a small article in an envelope and seal it. When they give it to you, hold the envelope lightly and try to feel the subtle energy radiating from the item inside. Try to silence your rational mind. *You're not trying to guess what's in the envelope.* Simply sit quietly while holding the envelope and be receptive to any images, thoughts, or sensations that you perceive within your body. Use all of your senses.

Have your partner record all of your impressions without giving you feedback until the end. When you feel that you've sensed everything you can from the object, open the envelope. Go over your partner's notes and discuss how the things you sensed may relate to the object inside. Keep in mind that the information you received may be symbolic rather than a representation of the actual item. Talk about the possible reasons you perceived what you did. Don't be frustrated or disappointed if you weren't right. The goal of this exercise is to heighten your state of awareness to subtle energy. The more you practice this exercise, the better you'll get.

Psychometry is one tool you don't want to be without in your medium's toolbox. Once you become skilled at reading the subtle energy of objects, you'll find that you're much better at reading the energy of people sitting or standing in front of you. From there, you naturally become better at reading the more subtle energy of your spirit communicators, which is the goal of every medium.

Chapter 9

Symbolism

What would you think of if I showed you a rectangular piece of white cloth with a red checked pattern? Maybe it would remind you of a tablecloth in an Italian restaurant or maybe it would make you think of a picnic. Now imagine that the cloth has horizontal red stripes instead of checks ... just a white rectangle with red stripes. Does anything come to mind? Maybe yes, and maybe no.

But what if I put a small navy blue rectangle in the upper left hand corner and filled that blue rectangle with fifty white stars? Suddenly, that piece of material isn't just a piece of cloth, it's now an object that you recognize as a flag. What are some of the thoughts that come to mind when you see that cloth now? Here are just a few things you might think of:

- The United States of America
- The pledge of allegiance
- Freedom and liberty
- A flag-draped coffin

Keep in mind that we started out with a simple piece of material. In fact, it's still just a simple piece of material. The cloth, by itself, has no particular meaning, but look at the different imagery we've come to associate with it by adding a few colors and a very specific design.

Now think about the way those images make you *feel*. Here are a few possibilities:

- Proud

- Patriotic
- Powerful
- Sad

At its most basic, a flag is just a piece of cloth with a particular pattern of colors and shapes, but it's the colors and shapes that turn the flag into a *symbol* with particular meaning for those who recognize the pattern. For example, if I showed you a royal blue flag with a white "X" connecting all four corners, it might mean nothing to you, but it would be very significant to someone from the United Kingdom.

A blue flag with a white X is the national flag of Scotland. Any Scot would see that piece of cloth and could have the same types of nationalistic thoughts and feelings as an American does when they see the stars and stripes. Interestingly enough, the same blue flag with a white cross has a completely different meaning for seamen not just from Scotland, but from any country in the world. That pattern is used on maritime signal flags to symbolize the letter M and also to indicate that a vessel flying that flag is stopped and not making way.

In its most simple form, a symbol is something that represents something else. Anything can be a symbol. It can be an actual physical object like a flag, or a character with no particular meaning by itself other than what it stands for, such as the symbol π, which is a representation of a mathematical number. A symbol like π has only one meaning. Many other symbols, like the blue and white flag, are subject to interpretation by each person who sees them.

Symbolism is very important in mediumship. All symbolism that is shown to us in mediumship is given to us by the spirit world as a way to help us identify either a name, a place, a situation, or a memory. If the spirit people realize they can work with you best through visual imagery, they will often use symbols to communicate visually, although you can have symbolic sounds as well. It's up to you to figure out if what they're giving you is an actual image or sound, or a symbol of something related to that image or sound. For example, suppose you see a bridge in your mind's eye. There may be an actual bridge that was important to the spirit communicator, or the bridge could be a symbol that represents some kind of transition in someone's life.

As with all forms of mediumship, the more you practice, the better you'll get at interpreting imagery. Start by taking each symbol at its face value. When you see an image in your mind's eye, ask yourself what it means to you. Once you've established a personal meaning for each symbol, the spirit communicators will know they can use that image again with you with the same or similar meaning.

You might hear a medium on the platform say, "When I see an anchor, it always means 'stability' to me." That medium has established a working link with his or her spirit communicator regarding what an anchor stands for. They can then expand upon that meaning to interpret whether stability relates to the person they're working with or the spirit communicator.

I've been working with the spirit people so long that they use some of the same symbols over and over with me. Any time I see an orange during a reading, I know right away that I need to talk about Florida. One of my strongest personal symbols is one of those yellow "wet floor" cones that janitors put out after cleaning. When I see that, I know to pass along some kind of cautionary message. Those cones are always a huge warning sign for me. If somebody asks me if they should do something or make a certain decision and I see a green traffic signal, I know that means they should go ahead.

A traffic light is one example of an archetype, or a symbol that's universal in its meaning. This type of image represents the same things across all cultures. A lion is another example of an archetype, symbolizing power and strength. A red cross is another universal symbol that's used around the world to represent assistance or first-aid for those in need. Archetypes can be useful in mediumship, but you need to be careful and not immediately communicate the accepted meaning until you've established that as one of your reliable symbols.

For example, imagine that you're giving a reading and you see the image of a dog. You may tell your sitter that you're seeing a dog, but they reply that nobody they know ever owned a dog. You know what you're seeing, so you figure that maybe the dog is some kind of a symbol. As an archetype, dogs represent "man's best friend" and "loyalty." But what if you or your sitter were bitten by a dog as a child? The image might represent completely different thoughts and feelings for someone who's had a bad experience in the past. Images can be deeply personal, and people can interpret them in unique ways.

Because symbols can have more than one interpretation, you'll need to practice a process I call *mind mapping* when the spirit people give you something. Mind mapping involves using your mind to follow the links to all of the symbol's potential meanings. When you see an image, say to yourself, "This looks like a (whatever it is), but how could I interpret this differently?" For example, if I see a rose, does that mean I should talk about the actual flower, or could it mean the name Rose?

If I mind map the image even farther, I might find that the spirit people are trying to get me to say the name Theresa. They know that St. Theresa is my favorite, and she is always associated with roses. Or how about if I'm giving a reading and I suddenly think of *I love Lucy*? There are three different ways I could interpret that. It could either represent the name Lucy, or a redhead, or someone with Lucille Ball's wacky personality.

When you get in the habit of mind mapping the images, sounds, and thoughts you receive from the spirit people, your mind will automatically map out the various possibilities. Remember this: The spirit people never waste a thought. If they send you a thought, sound, or image that doesn't immediately mean something to you or your sitter, map it out. There's always a reason you get what you're get. Always.

Say you hear bells ringing and you tell that to your sitter. If that doesn't mean anything to them, go on to another possible meaning. Maybe someone's last name is Bell, or maybe there's an anniversary coming up. Use the no's you get as an indication that you need to dig a little farther.

Often an image can hold not just one, but multiple messages contained within it, so it's important to look at all the elements of any imagery you receive. For example, if you see a gate with five bars, what does that mean to you? The five bars could represent a time span of, say, five years, five months, or five days. Look farther. Is the gate attached to a fence? If so, is the gate open or closed? An open gate could represent an opportunity opening up for your sitter during a time span with a five in it. If closed, it could mean that a new opportunity won't occur before that time period passes. When the meaning isn't clear, you'll have to use your intuition to guide you toward an understanding of the intended meaning.

There may be times when a piece of communication from the other side means nothing to you, but it could be a powerful symbol for your sitter. For this reason, when giving a reading or doing a demonstration it's important to share aloud whatever you're getting. Make sure that you state what you're seeing without asking a question. Once you've put the information out there, you can work together to figure out the symbol.

A perfect example of this happened during a reading when the spirit people showed me a spatula. This was the first time they'd ever shown me something like that, so I didn't have any symbolic reference. I simply said, "I'm seeing a spatula." Naturally, I thought of food. I wondered if maybe the spirit or the sitter had been a chef, but the lady I was working with didn't take either of those interpretations. The spirit communicator wasn't giving up, though. She kept putting this spatula down in front of me. Since I'd already stated the information and a couple of interpretations, it was then okay to ask aloud, "Why am I getting a spatula?" After all, I knew what I was seeing, and I can't say this enough: *The spirit people never waste a thought.*

My sitter then said, "Well, my last name is 'Spah-TOO-lah'"

Its times like that when you want to say, "Well, why didn't you say so in the first place?" But that sort of thing happens a lot. Sometimes it's hours or days later before they realize what you were trying to tell them.

I recommend that you take the time to study symbology in more depth. One of the best books I've found that can help mediums in interpreting symbols is *The Encyclopedia of Symbolism* by Kevin Todeschi. The book offers over 2000 interpretations of creative symbols. Go through it slowly and learn what the various symbols mean. As you see images in your readings or even in your dreams, look them up in the book and see if the interpretations make the images more meaningful.

In all forms of mental mediumship, whether the spirit world communicates with you through clairvoyance, clairaudience, or clairsentience, you as the medium have to decipher the symbolic images you receive. All things being shown to you will lead to a name, a place, or a situation. As I said earlier, once you see the same symbol once or twice and associate it with a certain meaning, it will become part of your personal toolbox of symbols. When understood correctly, symbols will help to give a clearer message.

Never forget that we are dealing with intelligence on the other side. Knowing that, we have to accept that the spirit world is going to show you the quickest way to get to something. They know what your personal symbols are and will use those as appropriate to get their point across.

I've always said that if we could use sign language and they could use sign language, we could probably send information back and forth much faster and more clearly. Until that time, learn the language of symbols and you'll make their job and yours that much easier.

Chapter 10
Mind Focus

I've lost track of the number of times I've watched a student medium give a really good demonstration, then suddenly lose their focus. They start out fine, giving some excellent evidence that they've connected with a spirit communicator. Then, you can almost see a little switch go off in their head as they allow their rational mind to push their receptive mind out of the way. The spirit communicator is still there, trying to get through, but the medium has lost the connection.

In mediumship it's absolutely critical to keep the mind in a receptive mode, which is not a thinking mode. A receptive mind is centered and focused, but when I say focused, I don't mean actively concentrating. It's more like tuning into a radio channel. When you're not quite on the right frequency, there's static in the speakers and you need to adjust the reception. There's no effort or sense of trying. That would tempt the rational mind to get involved. The receptive mind is passive … passively focused.

Once you establish a link with the spirit world, your greatest task is to keep that link. For this reason, developing mind focus is hugely important for mediums. You want to give the spirit communicator the clearest possible channel, perfectly tuned in to their frequency, with no static.

Static, in mediumistic terms, comes from the random thoughts and doubts that intrude upon the receptive mind. When you're new to mediumship, the rational mind keeps wanting to nose its way into a reading or demonstration. It tugs annoyingly at your sleeve and makes you ask yourself things like, "Am I making this up?" or "What if I don't get anything else?"

Students who give in to these types of thoughts will stand there help-lessly waiting for something to come to them, until finally they look at me and say, "I'm not getting anything." That's when I tell them, "You're right. You dropped the link a minute ago."

You can compare communication with the spirit world to talking on a cell phone in your car. Imagine you're driving along on an open road and the conversation is coming across crystal clear. Five bars. Then you drive into a tunnel under a mountain and within seconds you've completely lost the signal. You're frustrated, and meanwhile, the spirit communicator is on the other side saying, "Hello? Can you hear me now? ... Hello?"

That, to me, is the same as an unfocused mind. Just like having to constantly re-dial the number when you drop a call on your cell phone, having to re-establish the link with the spirit world is tiring and inefficient. Your goal is to find that still point inside of you—that clear signal—and stay there. Once you've established a link, you should be able to hold that signal in place, even if you drive into a figurative tunnel.

To give the spirit world a clear channel, your mind has to be clear: clear of all thoughts other than the interpretations of the messages you're receiving. Without this clean plate, as I call it, your mediumship will be crude and unpolished. Your task, as an evidential medium, is to develop yourself, constantly asking, "What can I do to make myself the perfect instrument?"

The rational mind is used to being in control. The receptive mind needs practice to learn to step into the foreground and stay there. Luck-ily, with good discipline, it's possible to train yourself to achieve the high degree of mind focus that's necessary to be a good medium.

Mind focus, like concentration, can be defined as the process of se-lectively focusing on one aspect of the environment while ignoring other things[9]. And that's exactly what you need to do when communicating with the other side. At any given moment in the day, an untrained mind will bounce from thought to thought, constantly changing direction like a ball in a racquetball court.

One second you might be thinking about what to have for dinner, the next second you're thinking about your friend's new car, and before you know it you've moved on to thinking about the season finale of your

---

9 http://en.wikipedia.org/wiki/Concentration_(psychology)

favorite TV show and how the electric company overcharged you on last month's bill.

Once you've established a link, you have to block out this kind of unnecessary chatter from your rational mind and focus on the images, thoughts, sounds, and feelings you're receiving from your spirit communicator. This may sound daunting, but don't get discouraged. It's possible to train your rational mind to settle down. In fact, we've already discussed one excellent method earlier in the book: meditation. Each time you enter the meditative state, you're increasing your mind focus. This may sound contradictory, since you're not supposed to focus on anything while meditating. But good mind focus means concentrating on one thing only, to the exclusion of all other thoughts. This is exactly what you're doing when you meditate while repeating a mantra. The mantra becomes the main focus of your mind. With your attention concentrated on that one word or phrase, the rational mind is held at bay.

One method I recommend for increasing your mind focus is to count backwards from 1000 by 3s. It sounds easy enough: "997, 994, 991, 988," and so on. But wait. Did I mention that if you make a mistake, you have to start over? I guarantee that soon after you start, your mind is going to start shouting, "Hey, this is hard!" or "This is boring. I don't want to play this game anymore."

If you want to be not just a good medium, but the best medium you can be, you'll play the game, over and over, starting with a different number every time so it doesn't get too easy. It's impossible to do this exercise successfully while thinking about other things. Yes, this kind of work is tedious and time-consuming, but I never said that being a medium was easy. The whole reason for doing mind focus work is to find that centered, receptive place and be able to recreate it every time you give a reading or do a demonstration.

There are any number of things that are guaranteed to distract an untrained mind, with one of the biggest being extreme emotion by either the recipient of your messages or from yourself. I will never forget a telephone reading I gave for a woman from three thousand miles away. I closed my eyes and right away I saw two little spirits—a boy and a girl. I took a deep breath and actually shivered. I knew this was going to be bad. I told the woman that I had her two children with me. She couldn't answer me. All I got was a grunt in return.

Then I tuned in a little more and sensed there'd been a really nasty divorce. When I saw what happened next, I had to fight the urge to hang up the phone and run away from the reading. Instead, I pressed on and told her what I was getting: that her husband had taken the kids for visitation and killed them out of retaliation for the divorce. Then he killed himself.

The emotion coming through that phone line was palpable. What could I possibly say to that woman? I could barely talk, myself, and a band of sorrow seemed to want to squeeze the remaining air from my chest. This was the kind of reading where a less experienced medium would have dropped the link from the sheer intensity of the emotion.

I asked the children to give me some details to show their mother that I wasn't just reading her mind. They really came through for me, naming their favorite toys and describing the bedtime ritual they used to enjoy each night with their mom. Best of all, they gave me a new image for their mother to hold in her heart: that of her two young children playing happily in the Summerland, as they called it, and blowing her kisses from a field of yellow daisies.

By the end of the call, the woman's voice had regained its strength. "I need you to know something," she said. "If you hadn't told me what you did tonight, I was going to kill myself."

I have often been asked about the amount of empathy we are to feel for our clients.

This woman needed to know that I as a minister I cared about her deep distress, at the end of the reading she was told there would be no fee for this session ,she was also told she could call us at the Church if she needed to just talk. Often you must respond to the heartbreak of another human's suffering with love and compassion. You are here to serve in your ministry as a medium, the spirit world has chosen you, serve well.

That's why practicing the exercises in this chapter is so important. Can you imagine if I'd allowed the emotion to overwhelm me and I hadn't given that woman the message she needed to hear? I realized then that no one other than a psychiatrist, or maybe a family doctor, has the kind of access to a person's soul that a medium does. My clients tell me things they wouldn't share with anyone else … things they keep inside, if only to spare themselves further pain.

Holding mind focus under pressure like that has to become second nature. It has to be part of the way you work, without even thinking about it, so you can function when things get rough. Many times I want to cry with my clients, and you may get that way, too, but that's not why people will come to you. If they need someone to cry with them, they can go to a friend or a counselor. They'll come to you for the evidence that their loved ones are still around. To know that they're okay. You have to be strong and hold your focus so you don't get into the emotion.

Here are a few other things that can throw the mind out of focus:

- **You're in a distraught place in your own life**. When your rational mind is distracted by personal events and emotions, the receptive mind isn't available and clear to work. I've known mediums who recognized this fact and decided not to give readings for a month until they dealt with their issues. I think that's an ethical thing to do.

- **Getting "no's" during a message**. New mediums often lack confidence. When they give a piece of evidence and either no one takes the message or they say "No, that's not right," the rational mind jumps in and they lose their focus. I wasn't immune to this at first, either, believe me. When people used to say no to me I'd drop out of mediumship and go right into giving them psychic messages. It's a lot easier to tell someone "You're gonna get a new job next month," than to hold onto Uncle Harry in the spirit world and listen to what he's trying so hard to get across. Remember: the spirit people never waste a thought. If someone gives you a no, it's not necessarily your fault. Hold the focus and stick to your guns. You know what you're getting.

- **Reading for people in a disturbed environment**. This can be very challenging for an untrained medium. I started out giving readings and demonstrations in the back of a bookstore. People were working and doing other things there, and that didn't do a whole lot to help me focus. Now I have my own church and that has made a world of differrence. When people walk in the door for the first time, many of them comment on the loving energy that you can't help but feel. Because we give demonstrations and readings there all the time, we've built a space that's really good for receptivity.

I once gave a demonstration in a Barnes and Noble bookstore. It was a pretty distracting environment, with customers who weren't listening walking past, but things were going great thanks to all my years of training. Then a heckler stood up in the back and began shouting all kinds of nasty accusations. I asked the man to leave, but he kept on interrupting. Eventually, security had to come and take the guy away. It was a pretty ugly scene, but because I'd worked hard to develop my mind focus, I was able to bring forth some tremendous evidence for the audience in spite of it all.

You also need to be prepared to deal with people who are argumentative or simply a sitter with whom you have a bad rapport. If your mind is untrained, that kind of person will throw you out of focus. If you're well trained, nothing will throw you.

- **Extreme tiredness**. It's very hard to hold a channel when your mind is fatigued. I've found that five readings in a row is about the maximum I can handle and still give my clients excellent evidence. The duration of the reading is as important as the quantity. I limit my readings to thirty minutes. Many people will want an hour, but in my opinion, with evidential mediumship half an hour is plenty of time to give your sitters all the evidence they need to know that you're communicating with their loved ones.

Holding onto the same spirit communicator for too long is also tiring. I once had five people come to me for readings, one after the other. I had no idea they were all related until the same spirit communicator kept showing up for each of them. I kept thinking to myself, "Oh, I saw this lady before," and I tried to give new information to each person. I went out of my way not to repeat evidence. At the end of those five readings, I was drained.

As time goes on and you grow more competent, these things should no longer throw you. For now, as a beginning medium, it's helpful to know why it is that you may be having trouble holding your focus. You want to always be in that place that gives the spirit world a clean plate to work with—that makes you ready for the spirits to start sending you information. If you're ready for even more intense training, give the following exercises a try. You can do them any time, no matter where you are, and you don't need a partner to practice.

Exercise 10.1

Choose a color in your mind. Set a timer for 60 seconds and begin to concentrate on the color you chose. See the color in your mind's eye as the timer ticks away. As random thoughts pop into your mind, don't resist them; simply let them float away. At the end of one minute, take a few deep breaths, then choose a new color and re-set the timer. Repeat the exercise. Continue to change the color and re-set the timer for as long as you are able to maintain good focus. Take a few deep breaths between each color. Finish the exercise by concentrating on pure white for 60 seconds.

Concentrating on various colors is an excellent way to increase your ability to focus for long periods of time. It also helps to develop your clairvoyance. If you're feeling especially motivated, you can continue the exercise and work on your clairaudience by moving on to various sounds. Be sure to take a few minutes to break the train of thought and relax when finished with your color focus. When you're ready to resume, focus on individual sounds, one at a time, holding the sound in your mind's ear for one minute each. You can choose any sound you like. The possibilities are almost infinite, but here are a few examples:

- Ringing church bells
- Hard rain on a metal roof
- A violin playing scales
- A piano playing *Chopsticks*
- Waves crashing against rocks

You'll know you're making progress in training your mind when the number of random thoughts which break your concentration becomes fewer and farther between.

Exercise 10.2

Take several deep breaths. Tense all of your muscles, then one by one relax them as you enter into a meditative state. When you're feeling calm and peaceful, visualize a hot air balloon in your mind's eye. Watch the balloon approach from a distance, then slowly drift to the ground in front of you. See yourself approach the basket and climb inside.

Turn and look outside of the basket and watch as the balloon rises slowly into the air. You see that you're over your home town. As you float along, visualize every familiar street, every house, every building. Fly over your school and the post office. How do they look? Travel along in the balloon, looking for as much detail below as you can see, for as long as you're able to hold your concentration.

This last exercise is especially good if clairvoyance is one of your strengths. It mimics how focused your mind needs to be when the spirit world shows you an image. With good mind training and focus, once you see a picture in your mind's eye, you'll be able to maintain that link and follow it, just as you followed along in the hot air balloon. Travel along with the images you receive, look closely, and see where the spirit people take you.

Exercise 10.3

Sit in a quiet place and relax by taking a few deep breaths. With eyes open or closed, focus on a red triangle in your mind's eye. Hold that image in your mind for at least one minute, then put a yellow circle inside the red triangle with the edges of the circle touching each side of the triangle. Now focus on the red triangle with the yellow circle inside it for as long as you can keep your attention there. Finally, place a blue square inside the red circle with each corner of the square touching the inner edge of the circle. Focus on this combination of three shapes and three colors for as long as you can, but for no less than one minute.

I've given you a lot of good methods here for increasing your mind focus. I guarantee that the time and effort you put into improving your skills will reward you with stronger links and clearer messages in your readings and demonstrations. The more you practice these exercises, the more you'll thank yourself when outside influences compete for your mind's attention.

You are the spirit world's instrument. Those on the other side need your mind to be as receptive as possible to be able to communicate with their loved ones through you. An active, distracted mind blocks your ability to tune into their subtle messages. Mind focus is one of the most important tools in your medium's tool box. Having the ability to remain receptive and focused doesn't happen on its own. Repeated practice makes all the difference between an untrained mind and a focused one.

Chapter 11

Clairvoyance

Everyone—mediums and non-mediums alike—can see images in their mind's eye. This is what's known as imagination. Clairvoyance, however, is not imagination. It is the ability to see actual spirit people in your external environment (known as objective clairvoyance) or to see internal images in your own mind communicated from a discarnate spirit (called subjective clairvoyance).

I see both objectively and subjectively with my clairvoyance, but this is rare. Don't be discouraged if you've never seen an actual spirit person standing in the room with you. This type of wonderful occurrence may or may not ever happen in your lifetime. Subjective clairvoyance, however, can be developed. If you want to understand how a medium perceives objects subjectively, picture a bright red apple in your mind's eye. Do it right now ...

Could you see it? If so, rather than using your two physical eyes, you were using your third eye to see. As you learned earlier, the third eye is related to the sixth chakra, or brow chakra. Located more or less in the center of your skull between your eyes and even with the bridge of your nose, this center of psychic energy has long been used to see images, symbols, and colors. By using the third eye, a clairvoyant medium can see images as if they were projected on a blank screen in his or her mind.

Subjective images may be wispy. They may seem no different than images you'd conjure up in your imagination, just like you conjured up that red apple. You'll find, though, that the images sent from the spirit world are far more lasting than those you simply imagine. If you make up a picture in your mind, it will be hard to recreate that same image over and over. If the spirit world sent you that image, however, you'll be able to recall it instantly in the same detail you initially saw it. After a while you'll easily come to know the difference.

Some of the greatest gifts of clairvoyance I've ever seen have been demonstrated through the work of spirit artists such as the famous British medium Coral Polge and my friends Rita Berkowitz, Karen Jacoby, and Joe Shiel. These mediums see the spirits so clearly that they're able to draw their faces in great detail. At the end of a reading with a spirit artist, the sitter leaves with an actual sketch of their loved one.

During her 54 years of working as a medium, Coral Polge sketched over 60,000 people from the spirit world.[10] She became known throughout the world for the near-perfect likenesses she drew of deceased people. Stephen O'Brien, a reporter for Britain's *Psychic News*, wrote that, "She raised the spiritual awareness of her audiences. Huge crowds of people sat entranced as, from out of nowhere, their loved ones faces appeared again before their tearful eyes."[11]

Joe Shiel's drawings often match a cherished photograph that the astonished sitter later produces from a pile of pictures at home. People who have crossed over to the other side are recognizable not only from their facial characteristics and hair, but from their favorite ball cap or the logo on a familiar t-shirt. In my mind, there's no greater evidence of the continuity of life that a medium can provide than an actual likeness of a loved one drawn on paper.

Faces aren't the only images a clairvoyant perceives. During a reading or demonstration, I ask the spirit people to give me something meaningful that I can share with a sitter. I mentally hold out my hand and the spirit communicator puts an object into it. Using all of my faculties, I'm able to see what the object is. Often it's an item that means nothing to me, personally—like a silver dollar or a flowery tea pot—but it almost always holds special significance for the sitter.

Note that I said "almost always." There are times when I'll describe what I'm seeing to a sitter and they'll deny that it means anything to them. That's when I shake my head and tell them they're wrong—that the spirit

10 http://www.tomjohanson.com/coral_polge.htm
11 http://website.lineone.net/~enlightenment/coral_polge.htm

people never waste a thought. If they send me an image, you can bet it's important, and I let my sitters know that. More times than not, after they've had a chance to think about the reading or to check with another relative, my clients realize what the image meant.

I'll never forget a reading I gave to the mother and the girlfriend of a young man who was killed in a car crash. I knew nothing about the accident until the man showed me the details. During the reading I told them that I was seeing St. Theresa, who, as you learned in the chapter on symbolism, always comes to me with roses. The mother insisted that she didn't know why I was getting that particular image. As I always do when people tell me no, I told her to just remember that I'd said so.

I went on to give the two women plenty of evidence that the young man was there with us, but at the end of the reading, the mother didn't seem satisfied. She told me that she'd been asking her son all week to give her a sign during the reading that he was really there. In spite of all the other good evidence I'd given her, she wasn't going to be happy unless I mentioned a gift he'd given her one Mother's Day that she still treasured.

I focused my thoughts, but found myself guessing. I'll warn you right now to never fall into that trap. When the spirit people send you evidence, it's important to keep your mind relaxed and let the images simply come to you. By trying to perceive a specific answer, you bring the rational, thinking mind into play, and as we've discussed, that breaks the link.

I finally told the woman that I wasn't getting the special sign she'd been looking for. She then told me that her son had given her a small box containing a rose that never dies. I couldn't believe it. She'd completely missed her sign earlier in the reading—and I told her so—when I described the image of St. Theresa and the roses. That's why you have to stick to your guns. Like I said, the spirit people never waste a thought, and they would never set you up to fail.

Some of the best evidence I've ever given during a demonstration or a reading has come through a process called *traveling clairvoyance*. This type of mediumship is sometimes referred to as remote viewing, because it's the ability to perceive recent or current information remotely. Andrew Jackson Davis, one of the icons of Modern Spiritualism, and America's most documented psychic, Edgar Cayce, used to use traveling clairvoyance quite a bit in their diagnosis of a client's health. Even if a client wasn't with them, in their mind's eye they would go to the client for remote viewing of that person's medical condition.

In the 1990s the government declassified documents from an experiment called the Stargate Project. This was a 20 million dollar research project aimed at finding out if psychic phenomena had any military potential. They conducted multiple experiments with remote viewing, including efforts to have the subjects describe military facilities in foreign countries. They had some good success, but the program ended in 1995 when they couldn't find any value for military intelligence.[12]

While remote viewing may not have paid off for the military, it can be extremely important in evidential mediumship. Traveling clairvoyance provides real-time information that shows the spirit world active in our earthly lives. When I'm attuned to a spirit communicator, I'll ask them to take my mind to a place that will allow me to provide evidence to my sitter that their loved one is still around them in their current lives. Imagine the impact of being able to tell someone that their father saw them placing purple flowers on his grave that very morning!

I have a close friend named Carole who comes from a big Italian family. Recently, when her daughter got married, Carole asked me to contact her mother on the other side and write down something to prove that her mom had been at the wedding. I asked Carole's mother to take my mind to the church and show it to me. She showed me images with Celtic knots and St. Patrick. I couldn't help but wonder why I was getting all this Irish stuff, when I was sure the wedding had a totally Italian flavor.

After I told Carole what her mother had given me, she was thrilled. It turns out that the priest who conducted the wedding was Irish. There was a Celtic knot on the linen at the altar, and a big stained glass portrait of St. Patrick looked down on the whole scene. I had no way of knowing any of this. Carole's mother had shown me it all.

The spirit people often take my mind to remote locations when I'm working on missing persons cases. I close my eyes and they show me images of places I've never been to. It's my job to figure out where that is. Sometimes it's like putting together the pieces of a puzzle. They give me live intelligence—not images from the past, and when it all comes together, even if the story doesn't have a happy ending, I'm able to bring the family some peace.

12 http://en.wikipedia.org/wiki/Remote_viewing

Just the other day in church the mother of a man in my congregation came to me from the spirit world. I knew that the man had just lost his sister. "I've got your mother here," I told him. "She's showing me that you were just cleaning out all her sewing stuff, and she's telling me you need to look under the rug because she hid some stuff there." I also told him that for whatever reason I kept seeing Cinderella.

He looked stunned and said that just the day before he had been cleaning out the house where his mother and sister died. He had picked up a basket of slippers (like Cinderella ...), then moved the rug and found something there that had been lost. I then passed along what his mother told me next: that she had seen how hard it was for him to clean out their things. She'd seen him crying, and she'd come through to let him know that she'd been right there with him. She came to comfort him.

Can you see how beneficial it is as a medium to view things remotely?

Whether using traveling clairvoyance or simply interpreting images from the past that a spirit communicator gives you, the more observant you are, the better. When you see an image—whether it's a person, a place, or a thing—describe it aloud in as much detail as possible. Then, while staying in that receptive mode (don't allow the rational mind to question ... just remain passively focused), look even farther into the picture you're seeing. For example, let's say the spirit world shows you a truck. Don't just announce, "I see a truck," and leave it at that. Describe the truck: is it a pick-up truck, a delivery truck, or an eighteen wheeler? What color is it? What make or model is it? Is there any writing on the side? What's inside the truck? Maybe you can even read the license plate.

In other words, don't be too quick to simply state what you see and move on. When you take the time to look closely and stay with every image you get, you may amaze yourself with the amount of detail you're able to see. More importantly, you'll amaze your sitters by giving them incredible evidence that their loved ones are still around.

The better your skill at observation, the better you'll become at describing the images you see clairvoyantly. Artists are trained to look at a scene and see details that most people never notice. There's no reason you can't learn to do the same. In fact, this kind of detail is critical in evidential mediumship.

Get in the habit as you go through your day of taking the time to really notice your surroundings. If you're out for a walk, don't just stop and smell the roses, stop and look at them in detail. How many roses are there? What shade are the petals? What other flowers are around? Are they in pots or planted in the ground? Do the beds need weeding? Look beyond the roses ... what else do you see?

Exercise 11.1

Sit down with one of your favorite magazines and leaf slowly through the pages. Every time you come to a picture, stop and imagine that the spirit world has given you that image. Ask yourself how you would describe it in a reading or demonstration. Look for details that you might have passed over if you hadn't been paying such close attention. Are there things that might be meaningful to someone, such as street signs or town names? Do this exercise over and over until it becomes second nature to describe objects and scenes with an artist's eye.

We've done quite a few exercises in the book that will help you develop your clairvoyance, such as those in the chapters on symbolism and mind focus. Any exercise where you imagine something in your mind's eye and hold that image as long as possible is beneficial. For example, whenever you have a few spare minutes, close your eyes and imagine a beautiful tree abloom with color. Stay with that picture for at least a minute. Each time it goes away, bring it back to your vision and hold it there.

If you have difficulty seeing images, don't dismay. You may be more gifted at one of the other ways of working, such as clairaudiently or clairsentiently. These visual exercises are guaranteed to help, however. As with all of the other tools of mediumship, you must use your clairvoyance to develop it, and the process isn't necessarily fast. The path of your development requires commitment and dedication, but you will see results, and it's worth every bit of effort you put into it.

Chapter 12

Clairaudience

Think back to the experiment you did in the last chapter when I asked you to picture a bright red apple. You pictured the apple in your mind's eye and saw it subjectively. Let's try that experiment again now clairaudiently. Say the words "bright red apple" silently, in your mind. Do it now.

The way you heard those three words in your mind is the way many mediums hear spirit messages. Information can come through in a single word, a short phrase like the one you just repeated, or in a long burst of thought. Clairaudience means clear-hearing, but since you're using human ears to hear the voices of spirit, it's not like talking on a cell phone. It's far more subtle.

Just as with clairvoyance, there are two ways to hear spirit messages. Mediums can hear the actual spirit voice external to their ears, complete with the spirit's own intonation or accent. This is called objective clairaudience. When a medium hears words or phrases internally, as if they're their own thoughts, this is called subjective clairaudience. The problem with subjective clairaudience, of course, is that it can be very difficult to tell the difference between your own thoughts and thoughts coming through from the other side.

When you're in the middle of a reading or demonstration, try not to ask yourself if you're making up what you're hearing. That can pop you right out of receptive mind mode and bring the rational mind into play. As you know by now, the rational, thinking mind is not the mind of mediumship. You have to learn to trust the messages you're hearing and pass them along to your sitter. What may seem like a crazy or insignificant thought to you may be a meaningful, evidential message to a grieving and hopeful sitter.

That brings up a point I want to make very clear: There have been many jokes about people who hear voices. There are individuals with mental problems such as schizophrenia who hear voices that direct them to do things. This should never be confused with receiving factual information from a discarnate spirit. The spirit world will never tell you to do anything that would harm you or others.

With my clairaudience, I hear the spirit people as if they're talking to me in a normal conversation right there in the room with me. The first time I realized I was hearing spirits objectively was when my teachers videotaped me during one of my demonstrations of mediumship at The Arthur Findlay College in England. There on the screen I saw myself tilt my right ear upwards as if I were trying to hear better. Watching that, it appeared to me that if I lifted my head, the whispering was louder.

I hear music, sounds, names, dates, and even addresses clairaudiently. If the message is faint, I often say, "Give it to me again," and the spirits repeat themselves or try to send their message in a different way. Don't be afraid to ask your communicator to help you out. With good mind focus you can do this and still remain in receptive mode.

True clairaudience is a gift. As we discussed in Chapter Seven, clairaudience is associated with the throat chakra, which is the psychic center of communication. The development of the throat chakra will help you fine-tune this gift, but for now, let's try a simple exercise:

Exercise 12.1

Sit comfortably and take a few deep breaths. Relax your muscles from head to toe. When you're in as calm and quiet a state as possible, imagine hearing the sound of a train's wheels rolling along a track. Hear the whistle blow and the sounds the train makes as it pulls into a station. Hold those sounds in your mind. Take a few breaths, then imagine the sound of scales being played on a piano. When you've held that sound for as long as you're able, you can move on to other familiar sounds.

You did exercises similar to this in the chapter on mind focus, but for now, simply pay attention to how you hear these sounds. They're very subtle aren't they? This is the way the spirit world gets its messages across to you. They can send you any sound you can possibly imagine, so the more you work with hearing various sounds, the better you'll be able to attune to actual spirit messages.

Chapter 13

Clairsentience

One of the most valuable lessons I learned during my training in England was how the spirit world can use a medium's central nervous system to get their point across. This came to light in the middle of a class demonstration that I thought was going well. I stood in front of our group, my focus intense.

"There's a lady here who used to do something with music," I said, squinting as I tried to see clairvoyantly what the spirit woman was trying to show me.

"I'm not quite sure what she's doing …," I told the others, "She's playing an instrument or something … "

In spite of my focus, I heard several of my classmates laughing. I looked up to see my teacher shaking his head and scowling. "Janet," he said sternly, "look at your hands!"

I glanced down and saw my fingers running up and down an imaginary keyboard. Even I had to laugh. "I guess she used to play the piano," I said sheepishly.

The same thing happened later during that initial week of classes. I stood before my group and said, "There's a man here who died in his 60s from a heart attack, and he's showing me something he liked to do with his partner." I had a good link, but in spite of my focus, I just couldn't get what the spirit man was trying to tell me. I was about to give up, when once again my teacher admonished me to look at my body language. I glanced down and saw that my feet were actually moving about as if I were dancing. With that visual clue from my own body, I realized the spirit communicator was trying to tell me that he and his partner liked to dance.

This lesson showed me how important it is to pay attention to your own body language when giving a reading or public demonstration. It's important to develop the mind to a high level of receptivity so that the spirit people won't use you like a puppet. Until my students get to that point, I often videotape them in class so they can see their own body language.

It's truly eye-opening for someone to see themselves putting their hands together in prayer as they talk about a spirit who they sense was rather religious. Until I point their actions out to them, many students—just as I was in my early days—are completely unaware of how the spirit world can animate their body by using their central nervous system. This light overshadowing occurs when the spirit communicator draws near enough that you actually feel them in your body.

Most mediums feel or sense some of the information they receive. This type of mediumship, known as clairsentience, is generally associated with the solar plexus chakra in the area of the diaphragm. Personally, I believe that when we're open to receiving sensory information, our whole body becomes involved in the process, not just one chakra.

While in the receptive mode that's so critical to your attunement with the spirit world, stay aware of not just how your body moves, but how it feels. What may appear as a sudden ache or an unusual sensation could have nothing to do with your personal physical health, but could, in fact, be an important message for your sitter. I recall one time when I suddenly felt as if my whole leg was gone, and I realized that the spirit communicator had been an amputee.

One way I use the gift of clairsentience is to physically feel the way the discarnate spirit passed to the spirit world. I'm briefly impressed with sensation in a specific area of my body and I then know that there was a problem there. I perceive heart attacks or emphysema by the sensations in my chest area. I feel pain in my head when a person passed from trauma to the skull or from a brain tumor. I even felt a tightening around my neck once when a spirit came through who'd been hanged. Naturally, these sensations aren't always pleasant, but they pass quickly and provide convincing evidence to the sitter that their loved one is there.

Clairsentience applies equally as well to the sense of smell, which is known as clairgustance. The term is not as well known as clairvoyance, clairaudience, and clairsentience, but this type of sensory information can provide valuable evidence for your sitter. You may smell a cologne that the spirit wore when in physical form or smell cigarettes if the spirit person was a smoker. If someone enjoyed baking, you may smell cookies or homemade bread hot out of the oven. If a person lived in an area prone to floods, you may sense the smell of a musty basement. If you smell fire, the communicator may have been a fireman or he or she may have died in a fire. There's no end to the creativity of the spirit people in using their focused thought-energy to recreate certain smells or memories that hold meaning for their loved ones.

Remember to not take the information you receive at face value. If you smell a rose, that could have something to do with the actual flower, but it could just as well be the spirit communicator's way of letting you know their name was Rose. I once worked on a missing person case where I smelled rubber tires. I told the investigators that there had to be a lot of tires where the missing woman was. Sure enough, they found her in a parking garage that was full of cars … and rubber tires.

There's one other form of clairsentience that's not so much a physical sensation in your body as it is a gut feeling about something. The term for this experience is "clair-knowing." While not a common term, the sensation can be very valuable in your mediumship, and you should aim to get to the point where you trust this sense of knowing without question.

For example, let's say I'm giving a public demonstration and three people raise their hands after I've given the initial evidence. If one person insists that the message is for them, but my gut feeling tells me it's for one of the other two people, I know to trust that.

In another example, I once had a woman come to me and tell me that her son had committed suicide. That day I had a *clair-knowing* sense that he might have taken some pills, but it was an accident, and I told this to the woman. I then went on to bring through other evidence that validated what I felt and knew. There was no way to prove these words that she truly wanted to believe, but the other evidence I gave her that day backed up everything I sensed.

In exercise 6.3 you held different colored pieces of ribbon or tissue paper to try and sense their color. De the experiment again, perhaps using scarves this time. Have someone wrap different colored scarves one at a time around you or across your chest while your eyes are closed and try to feel the color. The following exercise will help you further develop your clairsentience by becoming more attuned to your bodily sensations:

Exercise 13.1

Close your eyes and while in a relaxed state, imagine each of the following sensations one at a time for as long as you can maintain good mind focus. Take a few deep breaths between each one:

- Imagine that you're standing in an ice-cold shower
- Feel the sensation of your feet burning as you walk barefoot across a beach on a very hot day
- Feel and sense the wind blowing against your body, so strongly that it pushes you backward

Once you've experienced the subtle sensations of each of these scenarios, spend a few minutes thinking of how you might interpret them during a reading or demonstration. Each of the scenarios in the exercise, just like any of the limitless sensations you could be given from the spirit world, could hold a variety of meanings. For example, the sensation of standing in an icy cold shower could mean that the spirit used to like to take cold showers, or that they lived in a very cold climate, but it could also mean that they lived in a house without hot water.

For this reason, just as with images you see or thoughts that you hear, it's important to initially report exactly what you're getting without interpretation. Once you've stated the information aloud and it's on the table, so to speak, if the sitter doesn't take the message, then you can try out various interpretations of what the spirit communicator is trying to get across with that particular sensation until the message is understood. If the sitter never does take the message, simply advise them to remember what you said.

Never forget: the spirit world never wastes a thought. If that thought comes to you by the valuable method of clairsentience, learn to trust what your body is telling you.

PART III

MAKING CONTACT

Chapter 14

Systems

Up to this point we've focused on learning the basics of mediumship. By now your toolbox is packed with the tools that will help you to become the best medium possible. You've worked with psychometry and color interpretation. You have an understanding of auras, of meditation, telepathy, intuition, and what mediumship is and is not. We've talked about symbols, mind mapping, and the different ways you can receive information from the spirit world. It's time now to get to work, and you should be ready to establish your link with a discarnate spirit.

Before you do so, I want you to imagine for a minute an office where the same people have been working together for years. The staff is good at what they do, and they're comfortable with the office routine. Then, one day, out of the blue, the boss announces that he's decided to retire. He introduces his replacement: his cousin from out of state who nobody's ever met.

Suddenly, people start to shift about nervously. The guy looks nice enough, and smart, too, but he's a complete unknown. Will he be a micromanager or a totally hands-off boss? What will his communication style be like? A couple of staff members whisper back and forth that they hope he isn't a screamer. A few people wonder if their hours will be the same. Will they be expected to work weekends and put in overtime? Some of the workers are looking more and more uncomfortable as they try to figure out what the new guy's going to expect from them.

It's no wonder everyone is feeling uncomfortable. They're all so used to their routines ... With a new boss, there are so many new variables, and any one of them could have a major effect on the office's efficiency and effectiveness. One thing's for sure, they're going to need good two-way communication and they're going to have to figure out real fast the best way to work together if they want to minimize disruptions.

By now you may be wondering, what does all this have to do with mediumship? Let me tell you: It's more relevant than most people would imagine ...

Mediumship is all about communication, and any time two or more people try to communicate, there are bound to be misunderstandings. It's hard enough when the people who are exchanging ideas are in the same room. It gets even tougher when they can't see each other, such as when talking long distance on the telephone. So what do you think it's like when you're dealing with different realms of existence?

As I've stated repeatedly, we're dealing with intelligence on the other side. The spirit people know how difficult it is to communicate between our two worlds. They know that the difference in our vibratory rates is a real barrier to making their presence known. They know that for the most part their loved ones aren't aware of their presence, even though they're often around more than when they were alive. That's why they're so happy when they find a medium to work with. It makes the communication with their family and friends in the physical world so much easier.

The spirit people, just like office workers with a new boss, and just like you and I, are much more comfortable when everyone knows what's expected of them. The best way to eliminate misunderstandings and to improve communications is to have a system for dealing with the spirit world and to be consistent in using that system.

A system is a standard way of doing something, and that's the what you want when you practice mediumship: a standard, unchanging method. If you tell the spirit people what you want from them during a reading or a demonstration and you always work the same way, that consistency will lead to the best communication possible. Good communication will result in good evidence, and that is always the goal in evidential mediumship.

So how do you get that two-way consistency? You develop a system that involves always starting your readings or demonstrations the same way and always expecting the same kind of evidential information from the spirit communicators. You get the spirits used to working with you so that everyone knows what's expected every time.

I teach a very structured method of mediumship, and it's that structure that leads to my students' success. You may be used to practicing a looser type of mediumship, but trust me on this: the spirit people don't like un-predictability any more than we do. So let's start with the basics.

Making Contact

Some mediums can attune themselves with the spirit world at will. They can see or hear spirits without making any extra effort. Others, how-ever, need to make special preparations to communicate with the other side. If you fall into the latter category, don't worry. Having a system for making that initial contact will give you the confidence to know that the spirit people will come through for you.

You may hear mediums talk of "getting in the power" in order to estab-lish a link. This refers to their method of getting into that receptive state that's so important to attuning with the spirit world. You may wonder how you can be in a state of power, yet have a passive, receptive mind at the same time. The receptive mind is actually not meditative. It's an ac-celerated state, because the spirit world operates at a much higher vibration than the physical world. It's a heightened state ... almost hypersensitive, but there's a point of stillness there as well.

To make that receptive mind possible, you need to be centered. You need to stand in your personal power, which is what "getting in the power" refers to. You become your own little furnace, with your personal power— your personal vibration—turned on high. If you've done the exercises in this book and worked on your mind focus, you should be getting better and better at setting aside the rational mind and maintaining that centered, receptive, yet powerful mind.

What you need now is a system for getting into that state any time you want. How you get to that state is totally up to you. Some people get there by saying a prayer. Some hold their sitter's hands. Others need to medi-tate. Still others focus on their solar plexus or heart chakra and visualize it expanding outward to infinity.

With me, I like to listen to music to build my power and I use specific breathing methods. For over a dozen years I've played the song *Where I Sit is Holy* every time before I give a demonstration in my church. Some people might get tired of hearing the same song over and over, but let me tell you, it doesn't matter how many times I've heard that music, when those drums and the flute start playing, they put me in the perfect place to connect with the spirit world. I also close my eyes and take a couple of deep breaths to enter a light altered state.

If you're giving a public demonstration, you'll most likely be standing. In a private reading, you'll be seated next to or across from your sitter. At first you may be more comfortable closing your eyes so that you focus on the information coming through rather than on the people looking at you. I find it best to keep my eyes open, but everyone is different.

Your goal should be to use whatever method works for you to build your power, then you simply tune in and invite the spirit people to come to you. For me it's like flipping a switch and I'm "on." I don't change things around every time; I have a system and I stick to it. When I flip that switch, the expectation is always the same. The spirit people know what I want and they deliver.

For me, flipping that switch represents an ultimate abandonment of doubt and an absolute trust in my relationship with the spirit world. There's an energy that comes with that level of trust. In that moment, it's just me and them. The distractions of the room are gone. I become a complete and open conduit for them to work through.

You can expect the same results when you develop your own way of working. Don't let the spirit world wonder if you're ready. Have your own system for making contact, then stick with it. Consistency is key.

Once you're in the power, relax. Trust that the spirit people aren't going to let you down. Believe me, they want to make contact as much as you do. When you worry or show doubt, you're negating their presence. Don't let them down. Know that they've been waiting to find a medium like you to work with. Don't put your hands up in the air and think, "Oh, I hope something's coming." Trust that they *will* come through for you, then relax and have fun with your mediumship.

Name, Rank, and Serial Number

You've developed a system for making contact. You've gone through your routine, and you've invited the spirit people to come around. There's now at least one spirit communicator with you. You know they're there because you sense them. You sense a change in energy or you see or hear them. For every medium it's a little bit different, but you'll learn to recognize the presence in your own way.

So what do you do? Do you wait for the spirit people to simply transmit thoughts or images to you at random? No. You let them know in advance exactly what information you want to get from them, then you trust them to give it to you. I call this system "Name, Rank, and Serial Number." Following this system is guaranteed to increase your confidence level and to take the guess-work out of your mediumship for both you and the spirit world.

Here's how it works: Imagine behind you a cloud of mist. Imagine the spirit people stepping into this mist. Know that they are going to give you three pieces of information. How do you know? Because you are setting that expectation right now. The spirit world is working with you as you read this. They're aware of your desire to work with them. They are intelligent beings, and they will give you exactly what you ask. So this is what you're going to expect to get every time you give a reading or a do a demonstration:

1. Are they a man or a woman?
2. Were they young or old when they died?
3. How did they die?

That's how you start. Every time. You don't start with imagery or vague messages. You start with this basics. This information becomes your anchor. It's a beginning point that—like an anchor—holds you and the spirit communicator firmly in place rather than drifting about trying to figure out if you really are linked with the spirit world. The answers that you sense to these three basic questions will give you the confidence to hold onto that link and receive even more evidence for the recipient of your messages.

I have students who come to my class who had been practicing their own brand of mediumship before studying with me. For some of them it's hard to undo an unstructured style. Even though I tell them to start with "male or female," "old or young," and "how did they die," many of them still stand before the class and fall right back into the way they're used to practicing.

I can't say this enough: true mediumship is evidential. It's not vague, such as, "Your grandmother is here and she wants to tell you something." You want your gift to shine. You want to sit in awe of your own gift and think, "I can't believe what's coming through." You want your gift of mediumship to make other people sit up and say, "She must be talking to the dead or she wouldn't know that."

How are you going to get people to say that? By bringing forth the same type of solid evidence every time. It's never good to start a reading with fluffy imagery. You want to begin with irrefutable facts. When you start over and over with name, rank, and serial number (Male or female? Old or young? How did they die?), you set your anchor—you establish a good, solid foundation of information from your spirit communicator from which to continue working.

We'll cover the other type of information you can expect to get shortly, but before we get there, let's talk about those first three critical bits of information:

Male or female? The gender of the spirit who's made contact with you is the very first thing that you should speak about when giving a reading or doing a demonstration. There are a variety of ways this information can come to you. If you're clairvoyant, you'll see the spirit. If not, most likely you'll simply sense if the person is male or female. Male energy is distinctly different from female energy. It's something that's difficult to explain to someone who hasn't experienced it, but as a medium, you'll simply feel and know the difference.

Old or young? Those who've crossed over to the other side tell us that once in spirit, they enjoy their new surroundings and feel as they did when they were at their physical peak. Most place that age around the mid-thirties. When they work with a medium, however, the spirit communicator will help the medium to know how old they were when they passed, especially if you, the medium, have communicated to them that that's one of the first key pieces of information you want them to give you. The spirit person may show you themselves at the age at which they passed, they may tell you it, so that you hear it clairaudiently, or you may simply feel it.

The basic question you want to answer is if they died young or old, but the more detailed an answer you can provide, the better. One way to do this is by scanning the spirit person's lifetime in periods of 10 years. Try to sense in which decade of their life they died. Did they die as a child under 10 years old? As a teenager? Did they die in their 20s, 30s, or 40s and so on as you move through the years. The difficulty you may encounter with this method is that it's not always easy to tell a person's age even when you're sitting with them in the flesh. If you make a mistake in judging a spirit person's age and are off by a few years, your sitter may consider this a "miss."

If you're confident of the person's age because of the way you received the information, then by all means pass that along. If you have only a general idea, then try to narrow down the age bracket as closely as possible. Categories such as "elderly," "middle-aged," or "younger than thirty" are examples of ways to give your sitter a closer approximation of the spirit person's age when they died than simply stating "old" or "young."

How did you die? Once again, the spirit people will get this information to you in whichever way they think you'll receive it best. You may sense how they died through a feeling in your own body, you may hear the cause of their death spoken in your mind, you may see an event that took their life, or you may simply know the answer. If you don't immediately get specifics, you should at least be able to discern if the person died from an ongoing illness or from an event. An event can be anything sudden, from a medical issue such as a heart attack or stroke, or from some kind of trauma, such as a car accident, a plane crash, a drowning, or even a suicide.

Starting today, let the spirit world know that you intend to begin every reading or demonstration the same way. Ask them to always give you the answers to these same three questions every time, in the same order. Once they know what you expect of them, you won't have to risk using your rational mind to ask or search for this information. The spirit people will give it to you automatically. It's your job to trust that the answers are coming, and to get into and maintain the necessary receptive mode to receive it.

Once you've anchored the link with male or female, old or young, and how they died, you can move on to ever more detailed evidence. At this point, I ask the spirit communicator to step in closer to me. It's as if you're putting on their overcoat. That coat can have many colors, and it's your job to paint that person back to life.

I recommend that you write a list of any evidence you want the spirit people to give you during a reading. Of course you'll start with the basics we've already discussed—the name, rank, and serial number. From there, the sky's the limit as far as the evidence a spirit communicator could give you about their life. Don't be afraid to ask for the type of evidence that would amaze your sitters. The more details you can give people about their loved ones, the better. Here's a good list to start with. We already covered the details for the first three items:

1. Were they a man or woman?
2. Were they old or young?
3. How did they die?
4. What was their relationship to the sitter?

Is this a parent? A grandparent? A sibling? You may sense a more distant relationship, in which case you could be dealing with either a distant relative such as a cousin or in-law, or there could be no blood ties at all, merely a friend.

You can set up a system with the spirit world where you ask them to stand on your right side or your left side depending on what side of the family the person was on. Tell the spirit world which side you want communicators from the father's side to stand on and which side will indicate relatives of the mother. You'll feel drawn to one side or another.

5. What did they do in life?

Did they work at a desk or use their hands? Blue collar or white collar? That's a good place to start, but after that, probe for details. Once the spirits know that you want this type of information every time, they'll find a way to let you know. As always, you may sense the details clairvoyantly, clairaudiently, or clairsentiently. They may use symbols to get the point across. For example, a woman who lived in a time when it wasn't so common for women to work may show herself to you in an apron. This could be your symbol that she was a homemaker. The signs can be very obvious: if you see a truck, the man may have been a truck driver. Simply tell your sitter everything you're getting.

6. What did they look like?

Get as many details as you can: What color was their hair? Was it long or short? How was it styled? What shape was their face? What were their facial features like? What color were their eyes? Did they wear glasses? Did they have facial hair? Were they tall or short? Fat, thin, or medium build?

7. How did they dress?

Did they dress formally, in a three piece suit or dress, or were they more casual? A person's clothing can give you hints as to what period of time they lived in and what kind of work they did. The spirit world shows me uniforms all the time, letting me know if they were in the army, or the navy, or if they were, say, a policeman, or a nurse.

8. What was their personality like?

The answer to this question often comes clairsentiently. You may feel lightness or heaviness. They may show themselves to you dancing happily or looking gloomy. Were they a prankster or overly serious? If the spirit people know that this is the kind of information you want from them, they'll give it to you in whatever way you can receive it.

9. What was their character like?

This is different than personality. It covers things such as honesty and integrity. If a person was a scoundrel, that will come through. If they were the kind of person who would give the shirt off his back to help a stranger, you'll sense that, too. Were they courageous or timid, adventurous or the stay-at-home type?

10. What did they like to do?

Most people have hobbies or favorite sports. Ask the spirit communicator to tell you theirs. Remember: it's all about giving your sitter evidence. What could be more evidential than to talk about Uncle Bob showing you a pair of boxing gloves or Aunt Mabel holding a small plant and a trowel? Did they like to collect things? Ask them to show them to you. The question of what a person liked to do also covers habits: Did they drink a lot? Did they gamble? Did they volunteer and work with kids? Did they shine their shoes every morning? Did they bite their fingernails? There's no end to the kind of details the spirit world can give you.

11. What are some important memories?

The spirit people can be very creative with the visions, sensations, thoughts, or smells they send you to get across a memory that will mean something to someone still on the earth plane. I gave a demonstration in my church not too long ago and I kept getting these gruesome images: I was seeing chickens with their necks snapped. I couldn't help but make a face, and someone asked me why. Finally, I gave in and told the group what I was seeing. It turned out to be an important image for a woman in the congregation who had grown up on a chicken farm. Her loved one on the other side was sharing a powerful memory that held a lot of significance for both of them.

12. What pets did they have?

Animals that we've loved are often as important to us as family members. What I've learned from the spirit world is that love goes on, whether it's the love of a human being or of a beloved pet. Animals come through to me all the time in readings because they played such an important part in people's lives.

It's very comforting for those of us left behind to know that not only will we see our loved ones again, but we'll see our pets as well. They'll be there to lick our faces when it's our turn to pass over. In a reading, one of the most evidential pieces of information you can give a sitter is to describe a cat, a dog, or even a favorite parakeet that belonged either to them or to the spirit communicator.

13. What things were in their home?

Through traveling clairvoyance, the spirit communicator can take your mind inside the place where they lived. You can walk the halls with them, describing the furniture, the carpets, and even paintings on the walls. Was there a big fireplace with a mantel? What's on the mantel? Is the house cluttered or tidy? The more details, the better.

14. Where did they live?

This goes outside the house to the yard and beyond. They might have lived on a farm … if so, what types of animals or crops did they raise? Maybe they lived in a city. If so, describe it. Better yet, get the name of the city or town.

15. Have them show you a special photograph their loved one would recognize.

Evidential mediumship is all about details that you as the medium couldn't have known. Imagine the impact it will have to describe to your sitter a photograph of their loved one that they treasure. The spirit doesn't necessarily have to be in the picture, but it should be one that they identify with. Once you've put this item on your list, the spirit world will know you're looking for images you can share, such as who's in the picture, what they're wearing, and what they're doing. If you can give details such as a number on a football jersey or a team name on a baseball cap, all the better.

Ask the spirit communicator to take you in your mind to the sitter's home and look around for photos sitting on a dresser or hanging on a wall. If they don't recognize the scene you're describing at first, ask them to look in an album or ask another family member. Let them know that the spirit world never wastes a thought.

16. Have them show you where they're buried.

Not all cemeteries look alike. Perhaps the spirit was buried under a big tree, or there's a special headstone at their grave. If you look closely enough, maybe you can see the inscription on the stone. Maybe they weren't buried in a cemetery at all. They may have been cremated or buried at sea. Put this item on your list and the spirit people will let you know.

17. Have them show you some important dates.

This could be a recent birthday or anniversary. It could be the date they crossed over. Dates you hear could apply to the spirit communicator or to the sitter or their family.

18. Have them show you other family members who are there with them on the other side.

This is an important piece of evidence for several reasons: It's evidential in itself for bringing through names of relatives the sitter will know and want to hear from. It shows the sitter that the spirit communicator was met by loved ones and is not alone. Finally, it lets the sitter know that they, too, will be met by love and will be surrounded by loved ones when their time comes.

19. Mention any fraternal or military organization affiliations they had.

This could be organizations like the Veterans of Foreign Wars, Benevolent Order of the Elks, or any number of other groups.

20. Show you something to touch the sitter's heart.

This can be the same as a special memory, but it could also be a special object. I had a young man in the spirit world show me a flower like a petunia and I knew he'd given it to the sitter before he died. She confirmed that he had given her a plant while he was sick because he didn't want her to be so sad. The woman had planted the flower in the back yard. When she heard him mention it in her reading, it couldn't help but touch her heart.

21. Tell you about apologies and thank you's.

There are often things that the spirit people didn't get to say to their loved ones left behind, especially if they were taken very suddenly. Other spirit people might not have been able to express their true feelings when they were alive, but their time in the spirit world has helped them grow to a place where they're now able to do so. The chance to communicate through you, the medium, is a gift, because it gives them a chance to express the sentiments they otherwise could never get across.

Not everyone had the perfect parents. My father had a bad drinking problem and he didn't hesitate to use his fists. If a medium told me they had my father and described him as this really great guy, that wouldn't be evidential at all. My pop has come through to quite a few of my students in class who know nothing about my family's history. When they pass along his apology for the awful way he treated me, my mom and my brothers and sisters, I know they have a good link.

I've gotten plenty of spirit people who want to thank their loved ones for the special care they received before they passed over. Many were too sick to let their family know how much their actions meant to them in their final days. By putting this item on your list, you give them their chance to do so.

22. Validate decisions the sitter has made.

Many times in the final days of a person's life and often after they die, family members are left to make difficult decisions about their care, their belongings, and other critical issues for them, not knowing if they're making the right call or not. I've given readings to people who cremated their loved one's remains instead of burying them and never knew if they'd made the right decisions. Others were faced with the heart-wrenching choice of turning off life support.

When you as a medium can bring up a decision that you had no way of knowing about, that, in itself is great evidence. When you can pass along the message that the spirit communicator is pleased with the decision that was made, you've brought your sitter priceless peace of mind as well.

23. Show you scars and injuries.

This might not seem like a big deal, but let me tell you, it's huge. When you're dealing with people who're skeptical, a general description might not sway them. Bring up a scar that's hidden under clothing—something that only a family member would know about it, and boy, you hit pay dirt. Maybe someone will show you an old football injury to a knee or a shoulder.

I can remember having a spirit woman come through to me with scars all over her body. I said to the sitter, "Boy, she's had a lot of surgeries, hasn't she?" and the guy looked back at me with shock. His face clearly said, "How did you know that?" Of course, there's only one way I could know that: the spirit woman showed me. It helps if you add this type of thing to your list, so they know it's the kind of detailed information you're looking for.

24. Show you things they left behind.

Naturally, we leave everything behind when we cross over, but that's not what I'm talking about here. I'm referring to something special the spirit person might have left for the sitter that they may or may not know about. Often they'll tell me about a piece of jewelry or something that's tucked away in a drawer where nobody's found it yet. This type of thing is hard to validate during the actual reading, but I love it when my phone rings a few hours later from an excited sitter, calling to tell me they found the exact article I talked about.

25. Show you signs that they're around.

The spirit people find some very clever ways of letting us feel their presence. They can manipulate electricity to make lights flicker on and off. They can influence birds or insects to behave in ways that are unusual enough to catch our attention. They often validate the signs that they've already been sending to their loved ones that they're around, such as yellow butterflies or cardinal birds. Other times they'll alert their family of things to be on the lookout for in the future, such as finding an unusual number of pennies on the ground.

26. Show you how they're still present in their loved one's life.

This is similar to the previous item about signs, but it's the more evidential piece. While it's comforting to think that a butterfly or a cardinal was sent by a loved one, there's no proof in that. There's plenty of evidence, however, in talking about an event that happened recently in your sitter's life that you as the medium have no way of knowing about. When you can give someone a description of an event that they recently took part in, this lets your sitter know that their loved one not only knows about it, but they were actually there.

The spirit world takes me all the time to special family gatherings like weddings, graduations, and parties. In one recent reading a spirit man showed me his family standing at his graveside. He described them laying roses by his gravestone, then he showed me the sitter's granddaughter writing a poem on a piece of paper and setting it beside the flowers. The sitter confirmed that this is exactly what had happened at the cemetery the past Sunday. The family may have been grieving at the time, thinking that their loved one was gone forever, but thanks to this special message from the other side, they learned that he was right there with them the whole time.

Your private readings should last at least half an hour. How do you fill that time? You don't have to worry about it when you give the spirit world a list like this—they'll fill it for you!

Once you have your list, sit down and read it to yourself and the spirit world up to three times a day, just like taking a pill. You want to keep your rational mind from breaking your focus during a reading, so you don't want to be asking yourself, "What's on my list?" By regularly sending your list out to the spirit world, you're letting them know exactly what you want. No question.

Finally, the last item on your list should be for the spirit people to give you a message to pass along to your sitter. Why keep this until the end? Because messages by themselves typically aren't evidential. Anyone can say, "Your mother loves you very much and wants you to know that she's always with you."

There's nothing wrong with a message like that. In fact, it's one of the most common type of messages the spirit world gives us. It's a wonderful, loving message that will bring your sitters comfort, which is one of the major objectives of mediumship. Before you pass along words than can't be validated, however, you need to establish beyond a doubt that you are, in fact, communicating with the spirit you've identified. Following a system will do that.

How long do you read your list to the spirit world? Until you regularly start to receive the information you've asked for. When you complete a reading or a demonstration and you can look down your list and check off a good number of the key items they gave you, you'll know that the spirit world understands your system and is cooperating with you.

Because you're dealing with intelligence, there's no limit to the things you can ask them to provide you. Once you become confident that the information on your list will be given to you without having to ask during an actual reading or demonstration, feel free to expand the list to include the kind of items that will truly "wow" your sitters. Kick your medium-ship to the next level. There's nothing wrong with asking for street names, phone numbers, and even social security numbers. This type of detail may not come through often, but you're much more likely to get this kind of evidential information if you let the spirit world know what you want.

Communication between our two worlds is difficult enough. Systems make all the difference. Stick to name, rank, and serial number when working with the spirit people and make everyone's job that much easier.

Chapter 15
Altered States of Consciousness

As a medium, all of your work will be done in an altered state of consciousness: most likely in a light altered state, but some mediums go to an even deeper level for trance work. It's important to understand that we don't walk around in everyday life connected with the spirit world. Sitting in the silence trains us to experience the altered states that are so critical to evidential mediumship. Just as with everything else we've discussed, being able to access these states at will takes a commitment.

When you're fully conscious and alert, your brain emits waves of electrical energy that are very different from those it emits when you're meditating or sleeping. Using special instruments like an echoencephalogram, scientists are able to measure the frequency of a person's brain waves. The frequency is the number of cycles the wave goes through in one second. Brain waves have been categorized into five types based on the frequency: alpha, beta, delta, theta, and gamma.

This last level—gamma—has received the least attention until only recently when more sensitive instruments were able to detect them. This gives credence to what mediums have known for years about the spirit world: that just because we can't perceive or measure certain vibrations with our physical senses or with scientific instruments, doesn't mean they don't exist.

Gamma waves are the fastest brain waves measurable by man's instruments to date, with a frequency of over 40 cycles per second, In this state, the brain is hyper-alert and highly perceptive. You may have heard people speak of time seeming to slow down during an accident. Scientists attribute this to the brain's emission of gamma waves during stressful events.

In normal waking consciousness, the brain emits electro-magnetic waves in a frequency ranging from 14-30 cycles per second. In this state, known as beta mode, exterior stimuli dominate your thoughts. Most people spend the majority of their waking hours in the beta state, as this frequency involves thinking, solving problems, and taking action. In beta mode, awareness of the spirit world is suppressed—a critical point for students of mediumship to understand.

To connect with spirit, it's necessary to enter at least the next slowest level of brain activity. Alpha waves emit a frequency of 7-13 cycles per second. During meditation, your deep breathing, mind focus, and deliberate intent physically slow down your brain waves from beta mode to alpha mode. This is a much more internally focused state of being that allows you to tap into the subtle realm of spirit. This is the state in which most demonstrations and private readings take place.

Slowing down the brain even more, you can enter the theta state, where the brain emits waves in the 4-7 cycles per second range. You experience this state every day when sleeping, dreaming, and in that semi-conscious state just before falling asleep or just as you're waking up. This is a time when lucid dreaming often occurs—a phenomenon in which the dreamer is aware that he or she is dreaming. In this state you can participate in your dreams and change the imagery at will. Because the mind is in such a passive, receptive state when going in or out of sleep, it's also a time when discarnate spirits are most likely to appear to those not trained in mediumship.

For the trained medium, theta state is the optimum state for connecting with the spirit world through trance and trance demonstrations. The slower the brain waves at this level, the less a medium is aware of his or her physical body and exterior stimuli. In this mode mediums have access to what has been called the "collective consciousness."

The slowest level which humans can measure with scientific instruments is the delta state, with brain waves measuring less than 4 cycles per second. This is the state of deep sleep or unconsciousness as well as somnambulistic mediumship, which is how Andrew Jackson Davis generally worked. The specific development of trance mediumship usually involves higher levels of cooperation between the medium and the discarnate spirit, guide, angel or master (advanced teacher). The development of deep trance mediumship is a process of years of unfoldment and may never happen unless you have the physical make-up for it. For further development of this ability, look into the work of Steven Upton and Judith Seaman.

There are definite physiological changes that take place in trance mediumship. In some circumstances, when the trance state is light, the medium will recall all of the guidance given by the spirit and any conversations that take place. In deeper states, the medium's voice and physical characteristics change. The medium won't be able to recall any of the words spoken. All of this type of work is done with the cooperation of both the medium and the spirit. No spirit can take over a body at will and never without the individual's permission. A clear understanding of altered states of consciousness is imperative for the student of mediumship. It is to be taken very seriously. Its development and unfoldment cannot be rushed.

You may never work in trance, but it's important to have an understanding of the different states of consciousness you experience throughout the day and throughout your work as a medium. It's not too difficult to move from one state of brain wave activity to the next. You've probably entered into alpha mode many times without realizing it. Think of a time when you were driving a car and suddenly realized that you couldn't remember covering the last few miles. What happened is that you slipped from beta to alpha without even trying.

Lucky for you and for everyone else on the road, your subconscious mind kept the car in the proper lane until your conscious mind got back behind the wheel. This simple illustration shows just how easy it is to move our consciousness ever so slightly and be in a place where we can merge with our infinite self. Once you're in the light altered state of meditation, you can simply sit quietly enjoying the infinite peace, or you can use this time to contemplate a spiritual issue. Because of your increased receptivity, it's also the perfect time to talk to God, the angels, or your spirit guides and guardians. Remain still, listen passively for their answers, and allow them to guide you along the path of your life's journey.

Chapter 16

Spirit Guides

In the last chapter, I used the term guardians when referring to spirit guides, and you may hear others use it as well. In my mind, there's really no difference between a guardian and a spirit guide; it's simply a matter of personal preference. No matter what you call them, in evidential mediumship your rapport with the spirit world is hugely important.

Most of us are very comfortable with the image of a guardian angel watching over us—someone like Clarence, for example, in the movie *It's a Wonderful Life*. All of us, whether we're open to our psychic development or not, are watched over and guided by spirits who stay with us throughout our lives. They're usually spirits who have walked the earth plane before us and are now attempting to guide us in our journey here in this lifetime. Spirit guides are interested in the advancement of our soul. They, in turn, can actually progress spiritually through their role as our helpers and through their interaction with us.

Some people easily recognize their spirit guides during focused meditation – in that light altered state we discussed in the last chapter. Some guides are more elusive. It may take years for them to divulge information about themselves, so be patient. The first guide ever shown to me was for the longest time simply the spirit of a woman in a long, purple gown.

Over the years I've come to know many of my guides. One of them is an Irish woman named Mary. I learned about Mary's burial place in Ireland from a very powerful trance medium. Mary assists me in my readings when I'm especially tired. I'll say, "Mary, you've gotta help me out here," and I always know she's with me when I begin to speak with an Irish brogue.

I've had interesting experiences with respect to discovering my guides. I had the wonderful opportunity of having Coral Polge, the world's best known spirit artist, do a drawing for me. She's passed over now, but years ago she drew a native American and identified him as one of my guides. Sometime later, without any knowledge of the first drawing, another spirit artist drew the same Indian guide. The similarities were unmistakable, and most noticeable of all was that in both drawings the man wore the identical intricate necklace. Here were two different spirit artists on two different continents drawing the same spirit. The British medium Steven Upton had five independent people identify the same guide with him. One of the best ways to verify that a guide is real is independent validation by mediums who have no prior knowledge of your guide.

Some working mediums receive their information from their spirit guides. Others, like myself, receive communication directly from those who've crossed over with spirit guides assisting in the process. Every spirit communicator who comes to me has the assistance of my guide, who knows me, and who helps the spirit communicator to blend best with me.

An excellent method of developing a greater rapport with the guides who assist us is by doing cabinet work. A cabinet serves the same purpose as a sensory deprivation chamber: it's a device to help hone your skills in receiving information from the spirit world by blocking out external stimuli. The cabinets I've used are all made of wood, including the top, with a curtain or cloth over the front to block out light. Like an over-sized phone booth, they're large enough to sit comfortably on a chair inside without feeling claustrophobic. Once the front flap or curtain is closed, the medium can still hear and communicate with others in the room, but inside the cabinet it should be completely dark.

Cabinet work was done more often years ago, but it's still very valuable today for the development of mediumistic abilities. In my opinion, this type of work is for advanced students only, as it can be a very powerful experience due to the increased energy you're working with. For this reason, you should not do cabinet work alone, and you should choose only people you trust to sit in the room with you.

The group you work with is there to empower you. As each of you enters the darkened cabinet in turn, the rest of the group sits quietly and sends energy toward the cabinet. This serves the purpose of raising the medium's energy—charging their battery, so to speak. Inside the cabinet, because of the silence and the darkness, you're able to focus much more on your non-physical senses. The famous British medium Gordon Higginson's mother used to achieve the same effect when he was a child by blindfolding him and plugging his ears with cotton for his early development.

As you sit in a cabinet, your only focus is on being receptive and connecting with the other side. In my early days as a medium I used to do cabinet work twice a week. I did this consistently for eight years. It made a huge difference in my development. It greatly heightened the impressions I received and increased my relationship with my guides. If you haven't yet met your guides, cabinet work is an excellent way to help you become aware of the people who work with you.

As I said, cabinet work is for advanced students and requires a group to work with. You can attempt to get to know your guides at any time, however, simply by sitting in silence with the intent to meet them. The following is a simple meditation to assist you in this process.

Exercise 16.1: Meditation to Meet Your Spirit Guides

Find a place where you won't be disturbed for 20 to 30 minutes. Sit comfortably in a chair with your back straight and supported and your feet flat on the ground. Rest your hands on your knees and close your eyes. Take in three deep breaths, exhaling slowly after each breath. Relax your body from the top of your head to the tip of your toes.

Say a simple prayer of protection, such as, "I ask God and the angels to surround me with light and protection. May those who are here to work with me be present only in the light of love and purity."

Take another deep breath, exhale, then focus on your intention to meet with your guide or guides.

When you're totally relaxed and have stilled your mind as much as possible, imagine yourself walking along a beautiful path on a bright, sunny day. You see another path that goes off to the side. You follow the side path until you come to a bench and sit down. After a few moments of sitting peacefully, you notice that there is another empty bench across from you. Look at the bench and ask one of your spirit guides to come and sit across from you.

In this light altered state, become aware of the presence of your guide. Notice how you sense them ... you may see them visually; you may hear a name, or simply get the feeling of a man or a woman. You may also be aware of a predominant color associated with this experience. Whatever you sense is correct for you at this point. There's no right or wrong.

Ask the guide if they have a particular message for you. They may or may not have one. Remember that you are always in charge. Keep an open mind.

Spend as much time as you want in the presence of your guide or guides. When you sense that you've received everything they wanted to communicate to you this day, thank them for coming. Invite them to come again into your meditation and to make themselves known. Slowly begin to become aware of your breathing and bring your presence back into the room. Open your eyes. You may want to write down any thoughts or experiences you had during this time.

Whether in meditation or giving an actual reading, once you've made a link and are aware of the presence of your guide or a spirit communicator, imagine a mist behind you. Invite the visiting spirits to step close, into that mist. I've said this before: it's as if you're putting on the spirit's overcoat. When they step so close to you that you're wearing their coat, their energy blends with yours and you're able to paint them back to life for your sitter. I can remember giving a reading with a spirit from the deep south, and the blending was so good that I found myself talking with his accent.

When you've reached that perfect receptive state where you become aware of the presence of spirit, you are allowing their energy to blend with yours. I call this *overshadowing*, and it's exactly what you want to happen during a reading or a demonstration of mediumship. You want their energy to blend with yours, making it all the easier to receive their messages.

Sometimes the blending can be so close that it may get uncomfortable. In the spirits' excitement to draw near to you, you may sense tingling or other subtle changes in your body. If you find this unpleasant or worrisome, remember that you're in charge of your body and your mind. Tell the spirit people if you're uncomfortable.

I had a girl in one of my classes who got a good link with a spirit and she asked them to draw closer. The next thing she knew, her heart began to race. She wasn't comfortable with the feeling, so I told her to ask them to back off a bit and they did. This is nothing to worry about. The spirit people are simply experimenting to find the perfect blend with your energy. You want your own light altered state to be just right: not too deep and not too light. When you find that optimum state you can stay receptive to the spirit world longer.

Never forget that your guides are there to help you. It's only when in the presence of mental illness or when your motivation is wrong that delving into the spirit world may prove to be more harmful than helpful. When you come from a place of prayer and ethical responsibility, you should never fear those who come to you. Every day they offer us guidance and support, if only we would pay attention. Whether your interest in meeting your guides is simply to discover their identity or, more specifically, to have them help in the development of your mediumship, they are there for you.

Chapter 17

Healing

For most of this book I've focused on mediumship as a method of communication—as a way of establishing a link with the spirit world. In this chapter we'll take a look at spiritual healing—a form of mediumship that deserves special attention. Healing is the process of bringing God's universal energy through one person's body and passing it to another person. In that sense, all spiritual healing is a form of mediumship. In fact, some would say it's the highest form.

Most sickness and disease is the result of physical, mental, or spiritual energy that's out of balance. The clear, pure energy that flows through a healer's hands brings the energy of the recipient back into balance—into harmony—thus helping to restore the person to health.

Mediums should never lose sight of the fact that they are not doing the actual healing themselves. They are merely the instrument through which the divine healing energy does its work. Credible spiritual healers don't advocate using healing in place of medical attention; rather, they advocate cooperation between the two forms.

The healing of one person by another through prayer, touch, and the channeling of energy is an ancient practice. The Bible has many stories of Jesus healing others, but the work of countless healers throughout the centuries proves that healing is not limited to a few chosen individuals.

There are many forms of spiritual healing in practice today around the world with names such as *Reiki, pranic healing,* and *energy work.* Some forms involve actually touching the recipient, while others are hands-off, or may even be conducted at a distance. Spiritualists call their method *spiritual healing*, but the basic principle of bringing the body's energy into alignment is the same no matter what the form.

One of Spiritualism's most well known healers was Harry Edwards of Britain, who passed to spirit in 1976. Raised in the traditions of the Church of England, he was initially skeptical of Spiritualism, until he attended an open circle in 1936 which caused him to reconsider his views. He became an outstanding medium, and could have focused his energy on evidential mediumship. Instead, he made a conscious choice to use his gift for healing.

Thanks to the great media attention surrounding Harry Edwards' work, interest in spiritual healing soared. He founded a healing sanctuary in England, and to this day people from all around the world continue to visit there or call for distance healing. Harry Edwards and the people he trained have brought healing to thousands of people around the world.[13]

Most Spiritualist churches dedicate a portion of their service to spiritual healing. Guests are invited to sit on a chair or bench before a trained healer. The healer then simply holds their hands on or above the shoulders (sometimes moving to various positions around the person's body), and allows the divine energy to flow. It's amazing to feel the heat generated from a healer's hands. They become like little irons, and often the recipient can feel the energy flowing through their body like an actual current.

Channeling healing energy requires the same type of link as we've discussed for evidential mediumship. You, as the medium, are connecting with the same universal, intelligent energy or vibration as you do during a reading or a demonstration. In the case of healing, however, the energy comes from a higher source. As mentioned above, you as a healer would simply place your hands on the recipient's shoulders and say a prayer to establish the link.

The request of the prayer should be for healing to take place—for God and the angels to bring forth the pure, clear energy to bring harmony and restore balance in the individual. Should you choose to emphasize healing in your mediumship, I strongly recommend that you undergo formal training in spiritual healing offered through most Spiritualist churches as

13 http://www.sanctuary-burrowslea.org.uk/harryedwards.html

well as basic anatomy and the study of the chakra system.

I've had some wonderful personal experiences with spiritual healing. As you can imagine, as pastor of The Journey Within church, I'm very close to my congregation and receive a lot of requests to tend to their needs. One couple, Jimmy and Rita, have been with me from the earliest days of the church. Jimmy was the foreman for the renovations of our present building, changing what used to be an American Legion hall into one of the most beautiful chapels you ever saw. Jimmy put so much time into the job that Rita used to call herself a church widow.

I really came to love both of them, so it was especially painful for me the day that Jimmy came into my office in tears. He told me that Rita had been having bad pain in the back of her head and neck for some time, and that her doctor had sent her for an MRI. Those machines are very precise—the results are far more detailed than an x-ray—so it was no wonder that Jimmy was crying when he learned that the test showed a suspicious mass in Rita's brain.

The doctor told Jimmy, "I'm not a praying man, but if I were you, I'd pray."

Jimmy stood there telling me that he couldn't live without his wife, and it almost broke my heart. He wanted to know what my gut feeling was. I knew he wanted me to tell him that everything was going to be fine, but I was tired, and when I'm not feeling 100 percent, I don't predict. I told him I needed to sit with the problem for a little while.

I had to get a little distance from Jimmy's emotion, so I went into the chapel and I mentally looked into his future. As I looked down his timeline, I couldn't see Jimmy standing alone. That told me that Rita would still be with him.

I went back to my office and I told Jimmy that Rita was going to be okay. This is one of those times when, as a medium, you have to be really confident in your abilities. You don't want to make a prediction like that if you aren't as sure as you can possibly be that you're correct.

Next I called Rita and asked her to come to the church that evening at 7:30. Then I got on the phone and called in 10 of my church's top healers. When Rita arrived, we put her in a chair in the middle of our circle of chairs. Everyone grew quiet, and I opened with this prayer:

"Dear Father-Mother God, we come together today for Rita and Jimmy. We come to her in support. We come to her in love.

We come to her for intercession with you, asking for her healing—that anything that is illness be restored to health, and that anything that is out of discord be restored to harmony. We ask you to surround this circle with your love, and we ask healing angels to be present in this room. Amen."

At that point, I visualized a bright, white light and I passed that light to Sharon, my assistant pastor, who was seated to my left. Sharon said, "We pray for Rita and Jimmy. We pray for her healing. We pray for God to intercede." Then Sharon metaphorically passed the light to the healer on her left. We continued around the circle in that way, with each healer saying their individual prayer and passing the light. An outsider might not have seen the light, but to those of us in that circle, it was visual, and it formed an actual circle of light around Rita.

Each of us then got up—one at a time—and put our hands on Rita's shoulders. Later, Rita told us that at some point during the healing she felt a horrible, searing pain, as if something had broken through her head and come out. We didn't know this at the time. We simply did the best we could do.

I always tell people that you can't take things too seriously, and let me tell you, the energy was really heavy that night. I tried to lighten things up with my closing prayer. Jimmy still laughs at how I put it: "God," I said, "please don't let this happen. You can't split up Jimmy and Rita. It would be like Mike without Ike; like peanut butter without jelly; like Abbott without Costello."

That healing circle met on a Friday night. The next morning, at the doctor's request, Rita went back to the hospital for a second MRI—this one with contrast dye. (You know it was serious if they wanted to do it on a Saturday). She and Jimmy and all the rest of us had a pretty rough weekend as we waited for the results.

We didn't have to wait too long.

Monday morning the doctor called Rita. He said to her, "I don't know what happened, but there's no mass there. I don't know what you did, but you're fine."

When you hear a story like that—and when you're personally a part of it, as I was—I don't know how anyone can say that healing isn't real and that it isn't a gift.

Rita's story is just one of many seemingly miraculous stories of healing, but there really is no such thing as a miracle. Everything in life happens according to natural laws, all of which are governed by God. If healings take place, it's only because the healers were able to act as conduits for healing energy to restore harmony and balance to a body whose mind, body, and spirit were out of balance.

Healing isn't always successful, and because we're not privy to the bigger plan of all existence, we may not know why we don't succeed. Sometimes healing is used simply to make an individual comfortable when their transition to the other side is imminent or when an injury can't be healed.

We had another church member named Norma who we all knew was going to pass. She'd lived a long life and it was her time to go. We did the healing circle for her just as we'd done for Rita. We did it simply to surround Norma with love and to give her courage through her transition. Anyone who doesn't think a medium's work is sacred should sit through a healing circle like that.

When most people think of healing, they think of the physical aspects. Norma's case is an example of the therapeutic spiritual and emotional benefits that can be gained from spiritual healing. Recently I've been doing a lot of this type of hospice work for the great comfort it brings to everyone involved.

In one situation, the family of a woman who was soon going to pass called me to her home. The woman was still conscious. Her relatives and I sat in a circle around her bed. The family was Catholic, so we said the Lord's Prayer, including a prayer for the woman's well-being and for her loved ones' as well. I then began to talk to them about the family members from the spirit world who had come into the room to join us. I described the woman's mother, father, an aunt, and six others who formed a second circle around ours in spirit. They had come to welcome the woman to her new life.

At one point the sick woman's mother who had passed over asked, "Where are the red rosary beads?" I passed this message along, and someone got up and pulled the red beads from a nearby dresser drawer. The spirit woman then spoke of a picture on the wall that I hadn't seen until someone pointed it out to me. This evidence let everyone know that the family members were there to lend support.

These experiences are beautiful examples of the healing aspect of evidential mediumship. They move me beyond words.

Whether healing is physical, emotional, or spiritual, in all cases spiritual healing is done from the heart. You can see this at the healing temple at the Spiritualist community in Lily Dale, New York. Healers get up and provide their healing with no kudos for themselves. They do it simply to be of service, which is one of the main reasons we're here on this earth. Harry Edwards chose the path of healing because for him it was a higher calling, and so it is for any of us who undertake this sacred work.

Chapter 18
Private Readings

The reading by phone was my first of the day. A gentleman called and I went through my standard introduction with him. He didn't have any questions, so I started the session the way I start every reading: I flipped the switch ...

"I'm aware of a younger man who comes through," I told the man right away. "He says he just went to sleep, and I'm having problems breathing." (You'll note that the spirit started with name, rank, and serial number: Male or female? Old or young? How did he die?) I sensed that the young man hadn't felt any pain when he made the transition, and I told the caller what else I knew: that he couldn't have changed this outcome.

The gentleman informed me that I was speaking to his son. I advised him not to say any more, and went on to describe the motorcycle that the young man was showing me. The spirit made it clear that motorcycles were very important to him. His father confirmed that his son had hung around with Hell's Angels bikers a lot.

I went on to bring through the older man's mother, who had met her grandson when he crossed over. I told the caller about the hawk his son was showing me as a sign that he was still around. The man said that his mother was, in fact, on the other side, and that he had been seeing hawks around his house since his son died.

I hadn't yet established how the boy had passed, other than that he'd gone to sleep. Then I saw the cause: "I'm being shown Oxycontin," I said. "Your son didn't take drugs like cocaine; it was pills. He took several to get high. He says he's sorry."

The gentleman informed me that his son had taken some of his Oxy-contin pills, and they had reacted with his heart. No one had known that the boy's heart was enlarged. He went to sleep and never woke up. Then my heart sank when the man informed me that he prayed every day to die, just to be with his son.

"No," I said. "Your son says you have to kick butt for him." I used the exact words I heard, and I know they connected with his father.

The young man was clearly aware of my system, because he ticked off item after item on the list of things the spirit world knows I want to get, all of which were confirmed by his father: The son told me about his attempts to straighten out his life and get a trade and that he was going to night school to get his GED. He told me about a tattoo his father had that he wasn't fond of. He mentioned his Uncle Stephen, who was with him. He told me there was no marker on his grave. He talked about his watch that his father now wore. He spoke of a German Shepherd there on the other side with him. He mentioned his mother, who drank a bit too much, and apologized for not leaving on a good note with her. The father confirmed all of these details.

I had clearly provided enough evidence to let the father know his son was still around, so I ended the reading with his boy's message: "He says it's not your fault that he took the pills. You were a good father."

Then the man confirmed what his son already knew: that he blamed himself for his son's death.

I repeated the boy's message once again, "You've gotta kick butt and live loudly for him."

Later that day I received an email from the father. That short half-hour reading had brought him comfort beyond measure. He told me that nothing else in the time since his son's death had been able to remove the feelings of guilt and remorse he'd felt. But there, in the evidence his son provided through me, the medium, he was able to find peace and the will to move forward … to "kick butt and live loudly" for his son's sake.

Private readings like this one are my favorite way to work with the gift of my mediumship. Sitting for half an hour with a person who has come for a private consultation is a sacred time. Over the years I've given thousands of private readings, and I love these sessions. It doesn't matter if the other person is on the phone or in my office with me; for a brief moment in time I have the ability to bring back to a complete stranger someone they loved dearly and thought was gone forever. I get to straighten out misunderstandings and fill in the blanks—to pass along the words that people never had the chance to say. I help people to heal, and so can you.

Most individuals who come to you will have never had a session with a medium. They'll be unsure of what to expect and many won't even be sure they're comfortable having a reading at all. I had a gentleman come to me after walking into someone else's office for a reading. This other medium had some items out that the man didn't recognize, along with dim lighting and lighted candles. Right away he thought he was going to be conned, like the old days of psychics with the crystal balls.

Before the reading even started he was on alert. It didn't help that he had no clue what mediumship was all about. The other woman came to me and said, "I can't read for this man." I took him to my office and explained to him about our work. I had previously printed a page that explained mediumship, and I gave it to him to read. After putting him at ease, he relaxed and had a good reading.

We, as mediums, may only get one chance to have people look at our work intelligently. For this reason, the start of each reading should always be about putting your client at ease. Think about first impressions. Your office or the space in which you do your readings should be clean, comfortable, and welcoming. You want to earn the respect of those who come to you, many of whom are skeptical about mediumship, so put some thought and effort into this aspect of your work.

Have comfortable chairs, usually set across from each other. Put a small table near the sitter with tissues, water, and perhaps your flyers or business cards. You'll want to have a clock in view as well as a tape recorder within reach. You don't want the space to be too dark, but I also find that if the lighting is too bright it's distracting. Silence all phones and remind your client to do the same. Years ago I had a reading with a medium who asked me to wait as she answered the phone several times during my session. This is not professional at all.

You should have a standard introduction about what the session will be comprised of, whether you're on the phone or meeting in person. Welcome the individual and ask if they've had a session before. Even if they have, if their reading was with someone other than you, it's a good idea to go over what they can expect. As I mentioned earlier, you may want to have some printed literature for them to review while they're waiting for their reading.

You can tailor your introductory remarks to the way you work. I explain to my clients that I'm going to focus on the energy the spirit communicators are bringing to me and tell them about images I see, things I feel, and things I hear. I tell them that once I make statements, it's very important for me to get their feedback. I ask for yes's and no's, but not much more than that. I ask them to keep an open mind and I advise them that the person they're hoping to hear from most may or may not come through at first. Finally, I let them know that they'll have a chance to ask questions at the end.

Because I limit my readings to half an hour, I try to get through the introductory remarks rather quickly. As soon as they're done, I connect with the spirit world and we're off. I bring through the image of the first discarnate spirit who shows him or herself to me. I go right down the list with name, rank, and serial number, then fill in every possible piece of evidence they give me from my long list.

Always begin to move toward closure of the session five minutes ahead of time. If you've given plenty of evidence, make sure that you get a message from the spirit communicator to bring things to a close. After the final message, ask if the sitter has any questions, then answer them.

You want to stick to your allotted time for the session. Many sitters are more than happy to let you keep going on and on, but this will drain your energy levels. That's why I limit my sessions to thirty minutes. If you're well trained and you follow the systems you've put in place, half an hour is more than enough time to provide enough evidence for your sitter to know that their loved ones are with them.

There will be those who come for a session who'll tell you that the person they'd hoped to hear from didn't come through. You can try to reach for this information if time allows. Sometimes a client comes hoping to spend the whole session with one spirit communicator, and those who've crossed over surprise them by bringing forward someone else. You need to trust that those on the other side know what they're doing.

I remember a couple who came for a reading and the wife's family came through very strongly. A year later they had another reading with the same results. The third year the gentleman came by himself, and this time his mother in spirit came through for the whole session. He told me later that she was the one he'd been hoping to hear from all along. I believe this unfolded exactly as it was supposed to.

While giving a reading is a positive thing because of the healing it brings and the understanding about the continuity of life, unfortunately, there are many times when a client has lost someone tragically. They may still be dealing with grief and other unresolved issues. They may have unanswered questions. It's vitally important that you handle these type of private sessions with care and compassion. I recommend that you study books on death, dying, and the grieving process to be able to better help your clients.

I certainly needed a full dose of compassion in the days following September 11, 2001. Many of the victims' families lived in the area around my office, and within days of the terrorists' attack my phone began to ring. This was one of those times when I needed to be sure that people didn't get their hopes up too high about hearing so soon from their loved ones.

I believe that when there's a tragic, sudden death, there's a period of several days of settling in on the other side. Many who came to see me those first several weeks after 9/11 weren't greeted at first by the one they'd lost that day, but there were plenty who did come through. Every person who crossed over on that day told me of being immediately surrounded by love and being greeted by those who had passed before them. As the phone rang again and again in the aftermath of that crisis, we attempted to comfort everyone who called and charged no fee for those sessions.

I've had whole families come for a private reading. One of the hardest was a woman who came in search of her son who disappeared in the twin towers in New York City. I first brought through the woman's father, then her mother, and then her son, Joseph—the one she was looking for. The woman sat there across from me and shook her head when I brought him through.

"Oh no," she said, "My son isn't dead. He's just missing. I thought you might know where he is ... if he's lost his memory ... where we can find him."

My heart broke for this woman who wasn't ready to hear that her son had passed that day, but there have been hundreds of stories like hers. People's hearts are fragile, but fortunately, the human spirit is strong and love conquers all, even death.

One woman who lost her husband on 9/11 comes to me every year with her three daughters. They come just to see what her husband and the girl's father has to say about their lives and their decisions … to share some memories and laughs and to dream. It's times like those that help to balance out the really tough readings.

Many times in a private reading a small child will come through. Children are always accompanied by another relative. It's important that you identify both the child and the relative to the sitter so that they know the child is not alone on the other side.

Not too long ago a woman came to me for a private session. As I began the reading her mother came through very evidentially, with a great amount of love. As I closed my eyes again the next image I saw was of a five year old girl. The minute I described her and saw the woman's reaction, I knew it was her child. My heart sank, because readings where a parent has lost a child are always tough.

Luckily, the little girl made it easier for both of us. I spent the rest of the session talking about things that had been important to both of them. The child showed me trips they'd taken, beloved pets, and favorite toys. Unfortunately, the girl had been quite sick at the end of her life on earth, and I could feel the mother holding her in her arms as she died. I went on to describe the funeral, the headstone, and pictures left behind as the little girl showed them to me. As painful as all of this was for the mother to hear, it was especially evidential to hear about it from me, a complete stranger.

The mother described the five years she had with her only daughter as a streak of love in her life. I could see that she was comforted to hear that her daughter was fine now and in no more pain—that she was met by her grandmother, and that she was surrounded by love.

Many have said to me, "How can they say they're okay? They're dead. That's not okay." I tell them that there are two things that every human experiences in this lifetime: birth and death. Dying is inevitable. The manner in which one dies, the age, and how painful death is are variables, but the end of this road will come. Then I point out that the evidence I bring through shows that death is merely a doorway to a greater existence. No matter how one dies, no matter how one lives their life, we are accompanied in this transition. I remind my clients that they will see their loved ones again when they make the transition themselves.

Most religions believe in an afterlife. I have a strong Spiritualist belief in what the next stage of life is like and I often share it with those who are interested. The fact that life is eternal is a very important point to make at some point in every reading. Yes, we want to amaze our clients with the evidence. Yes, we even want to wow ourselves with the information we bring through, but the whole point of evidential mediumship is not to amaze people: it's to show the continuity of life. It's to provide an over-whelming body of evidence that all of us go on to another existence beyond this earthly one. That's why this is such sacred and important work.

No two readings are ever alike. Some will come to you who will be very interested in such questions as, "Where do we go from here? What are our loved ones doing on the other side? Do they miss us?" It's the op-portunity to help people understand the answers to these questions that makes private readings so special.

You will have sessions where just one spirit communicator comes through and will take up the whole reading. There will be others when a whole line of spirit loved ones will show themselves one by one. There will also be the rare occasion when you'll get nothing for your client. It's best to set a policy that if in the first ten minutes of the reading either you or the sitter doesn't feel the session is being productive, then you can end it with no fee.

You may occasionally feel that you can't read for a client. This could be due to a number of reasons, including your frame of mind, how tired you are, the reader's attitude, or anything else that makes it difficult for you as the medium to feel open and loving and to establish a strong link with the other side. In cases such as these, it's best to simply say, "I don't think I'm the right reader for you," and terminate the reading.

The ten-minute-rule is a good one to follow any time things aren't go-ing well. It's not in anyone's best interest to keep going if you keep getting no's. If you bring through a spirit communicator and the sitter doesn't acknowledge that they know who you're talking about, shift to the next communicator. If you keep getting no's with subsequent communicators, you know the reading's not going to open up. If all of your communicators are failing, you have to say to yourself, "This just isn't working."

There will be times, however, when you absolutely know you're right about what you're giving your sitters in spite of their refusal to accept what you're saying. In these cases you should fight your corner. Go back to infinite intelligence and ask them to show you how to bring this person through another way.

Rather than a set "three no's and you're out" policy, I advise you to follow your own intuition whether to proceed or not. The following are problems you may run into during private readings:

- Tough sitters.

  You may have clients who sit across from you with their arms and legs crossed. Some are closed-minded or are the "prove it to me" types who refuse to react to what you say. They'll sit there and listen to you give great evidence, but won't say a word. This kind of behavior is abusive and they become a block to their reading going well. This is definitely a case where the ten-minute rule applies.

  Keep in mind, however, that sometimes body language that appears to be defiance can actually come from fear. You'll know within a few minutes by the way they react to what you give them if the closed-off client is simply cautious or if they're the type of sitter mentioned in the previous paragraph.

  There are people who'll come to you who have no boundaries. They may be pushy and will try to keep you going after the allotted time. Long readings tax your energy, so stick to your schedule. Others may be truly defiant, leaving you to wonder why they came for a reading in the first place. You need to have discipline to work with people like this and terminate the reading if you can't shift them to be a supportive participant.

  Others may ask inappropriate questions. I've had people ask me things such as, "Was I sexually abused by my grandfather who's in the spirit world now?" or "Can my dead husband tell you if he was cheating on me?" You may also be asked ethical questions such as, "Can you ask my mother in the spirit world if I should abort my baby?" I simply tell these people that I don't ask those kinds of questions of the spirit world. That's not what mediumship is about.

- People beyond your ability to help. Some sitters may have emotional problems that you shouldn't attempt to deal with unless you are a trained counselor. If you sense that someone is suicidal based on their grief, you should have the phone number of a trustworthy counselor close at hand to give to them.

- Added pressure. While, in theory, all sitters should be the same, there are times when you'll feel the need to "perform" or put on an especially good "show." Mediumship should never be about performing, but in some circumstances you will be expected to demonstrate your gifts for someone who's not the average sitter.

A prime example is the day a reporter from the local newspaper came for a reading. She had already set the stage that she was expecting big things. Giving readings to members of the press always brings additional pressure. With that particular woman I wanted as little feedback from her as possible during the reading so that she couldn't say that I got hints from her. Even though I felt a bit stressed, I went forward with the reading, and I'm happy to say that her write-up was extremely good. Know what you're capable of, trust the spirit world to give you what you need, and proceed with confidence.

- Poor energy. Energy levels can make the difference between a so-so reading and a "wow" reading. If giving a reading is flat, hard work, and you're getting lots of no's, it could be due to you, the recipient, or your spirit communicators not having a good connection. The communication that takes place between the two worlds is very much like a cell phone signal: some days you have "five bars" and other days the signal goes in and out. You'll know after only a few minutes how good the connection is, and it could have nothing to do with you. There are so many variables that have to come together. Every reading is an experiment, and it's acceptable to have an off day.

If I have a day with consistently difficult readings, there's usually something going on with my energy. I may simply be too tired to do well. Some days every reading is a "wow" because all of the components—me, the spirit communicator, and the recipient—all just combine our energy perfectly. Those days are magical. Then there are others that will leave me asking, "How can I be so brilliant one day and mediocre the next?" Some days it's just that way.

You have to learn what works best for you. If you're struggling in your private readings, stop and figure out what's going wrong. If you can't identify the problem, you shouldn't be giving readings. You could simply need a break, or it may be that you need more training. One of the greatest suggestions I can give the developing medium is to offer free readings for at least several months until you're feeling confident about all aspects of conducting private readings.

If the problem is identifiable and temporary, don't be afraid to move on to the next reading. If you come out of a reading that for you was unsettling or disturbing, you simply have to make a greater effort to refocus yourself. After every reading you should take the time to step out of the energy from the reading you just finished. You have to clean the slate so you can start fresh. To clear the air, use the empowerment tools you use to build your power, such as meditation, a special song, a prayer, or chanting. Once you're ready, welcome your next client and prepare to "wow" them, but even more importantly: to comfort them.

Your clients may run the gamut of society. I've had doctors, lawyers, diplomats, celebrities, and because of my background, nuns and priests come to me hoping to hear something to confirm their belief that we go on and that love doesn't die. Many arrive with a bit of skepticism and a huge dose of hope. Because I choose to practice evidential mediumship, most leave with a whole new view of this world and the one beyond it. Appendix A includes samples of some of the many thanks I've received from those whose lives are changed forever because of the messages of hope I bring through from the other side.

Never let monetary gain influence your success or stop you from seeing someone in need who can't afford to see you. I had a man and woman come for a private reading after I brought through several of their family members during a public demonstration in my church. I sensed at that initial demonstration that there was a spirit communicator who was there but holding back. I felt she knew that if she came through in a public setting it would be too upsetting for the couple.

That spirit turned out to be the couple's daughter who had died at a young age from cancer. She came through very evidentially during a subsequent private session in my office. The mother and father were clearly stunned by the evidence I brought through that their daughter was still around them and doing well on the other side.

By the end of their reading, the couple looked dazed. I asked if they were okay to drive. They assured me they'd be fine, then thanked me, and turned to go. They were halfway down the hallway when the man stopped and said, "We forgot to pay you."

His wife looked stricken and started rummaging through her purse.

"It's not about the money," I said with a wave. "I don't need it. I just need you to believe in what I'm doing."

That couple—who previously had no knowledge of Spiritualism—came to believe very strongly in life after death and in the ability to communicate with those on the other side, thanks to the readings they had with me. They believed in what I was doing so much, in fact, that they gave me the money to buy the building for my church.

If your goal is to give private readings, you have to love what you do, for you will be an ambassador for the spirit world. Those who've crossed over are as excited about making this connection as we here on earth are. Never forget that you're giving your readings for both sides: for your sitter and for their loved ones in spirit. As a medium, you are their link with those they left behind. It's an awesome responsibility and a very special gift to be able to serve both worlds. Never try and force your beliefs on anyone you cannot convince anyone life goes on, but you can give them a personal experience that may end up changing their whole belief system.

I mentioned earlier that private readings are my favorite way of working with mediumship. As you develop your practice, be very cognizant of your client – of their emotional needs, their well-being, and of any brokenness. Be aware of whatever they may need as they leave your session, such as grief counseling, other professional counseling, or medical attention. As a fellow soul on this planet, care and compassion are at the heart of what we do.

Chapter 19
Public Demonstrations

When you consider that public speaking is the number one fear of the general population, it's no wonder that many mediums have some trepidation when it comes to public demonstrations of mediumship. It's one thing to stand before a group with notes in hand or to have your remarks well prepared in advance. It's another thing altogether to address a roomful of strangers without having any idea what's going to come out of your mouth, relying totally on your gifts, your training, and your link with the spirit world.

So why would a medium do public demonstrations? Because they allow you to touch more lives at one time.

Public demonstrations of mediumship can take place anywhere: in a Spiritualist church, in a metaphysical bookstore, in a public auditorium, or perhaps in an ongoing development circle in someone's home. No matter what the setting, just as with private readings, you should appear professional at all times. People will pay attention to everything about you: the way you look, the way you dress, the way you carry yourself, and the way you speak.

All mediums will find that they are usually more talented at either private readings or public demonstrations. It takes courage and a lot of faith to stand before a group of people and demonstrate your gifts. One of the biggest problems with this type of work is that the student gets up in front of a group before they're ready. This can have very negative effects on both the medium and the audience. Remember: don't run before you can walk.

You get only one chance to make a good first impression. It would be better for you to wait until you're ready than to rush to be in the public eye.

When you first start doing public demonstrations, simply getting up on the platform can be daunting. You have to deal with a number of components each time you give a demonstration:

- Your training
- Your confidence level at being in front of large groups
- How you're feeling on any given day
- The receptivity of the audience
- The energy in the room
- The power of the spirit communicator

That's a lot to assimilate, and you want it all to come together perfectly. I like to say that it's like mixing the perfect cocktail, and it takes a while to be able to mix all the ingredients just right.

For this reason, I strongly recommend that when you're new to public demonstrations, that you get up in front of the group, give a few brief pieces of evidence, then get off the platform. If you stay too long in the beginning and you have trouble—that is, if you run before you can walk—you may fall so hard that you might not want to get back out there and try again.

Just as with private readings, you have to build your power before you begin. All public demonstrations involve two aspects: the building of power and entering a light altered state. For this reason, it's vitally important that you come to know and recognize the altered state in which you demonstrate your mediumship. Each medium is different, and this will come to you by practice and experience.

As I mentioned earlier, one way I build my power is to put on my power-building song, *Where I Sit is Holy*. I do my deep breathing and I start to sway. This helps me enter that altered state. There are other mediums who sit down and pray to enter their perfect state. Whatever method you settle on, do it every time before you begin a public demonstration, then step up and work with confidence.

Always educate the group you're addressing about mediumship, about what your intent is, and that this is an experimental experience. Each time I begin a demonstration of mediumship, I lay out certain guidelines:

- That people remain seated
- That they remain quiet and be non-disruptive
- That they respond with simple yes's and no's regarding the information I'm giving them.

You should always begin your demonstration the same way. You'll make the link with the spirit world and provide the basic pieces: Man or woman? Old or young? How did they die? For example, "I have a woman here in spirit, she died of breast cancer at around age 60. This comes to me as a mother would feel, and I feel that she died at home. How many here can take this information?"

This is the critical question that makes a public demonstration different than a private reading. The answer to the question about who is the recipient could come from anyone. At this point, you may have more than one hand go up. You'll then go on to get more information from the spirit, such as, "This woman makes me aware that she lived in Brooklyn, New York, and worked in a bakery." These extra details will narrow down who in the audience is the recipient of the message. Once you're sure who the spirit belongs with, you continue on with more evidential evidence, ending with their message, whether it's one of encouragement, love, or perhaps even an apology.

This way of linking your spirit communicator with someone in a group is very strong, but there's another way of working in a group setting. It's possible to focus briefly on one person in the room and ask for your spirit helpers to bring forward someone in spirit who belongs to this person. You would then outline again the basic information and move on to the details.

No matter which method you use, it's very important that you remain in charge of your demonstration. Many times the recipient will be so excited to hear from their loved one that they will begin to tell you all about them. Do not allow this to happen! It's not helpful to be given information in any setting, but especially not in public readings. You may be dealing with skeptics in the room who can later claim that you were given all the details. Simply remind the recipient that you do need the sound of their voice as an anchor, but ask them to respond with yes's, no's, and no more.

If you begin to get too many no's, you need to figure out what's wrong. There are several options: you could have gone to the wrong recipient or you may have dropped your link and picked up a new communicator. At that point, you should back-track to where your last yes was and ask the spirit world for more information from that point. If your recipient still can't place the information, move on to a new communicator.

By the time you get to be a competent medium with all the tools in your box, you know exactly what's going well and can make a conscious choice to end the demonstration, if necessary, and come back another time. No matter how the demonstration goes—even if you feel sick to your stomach from nervousness—you always want to appear calm, collected, and confident.

The Janet Nohavec way of mediumship, as taught to me by my British mentors, is to always come off smelling like a rose. You strive to be as competent as you can possibly be and you reflect that by being totally polished. Even if your demonstration isn't going well, you train yourself to work with graciousness and with complete self-assurance. You want to always come across as a professional. Even if inside your confidence is lagging, you never let it show. Always leave things on a high note.

In a public demonstration, you should be mindful of the audience at all times. If you're going to harness the power of the room, you want to keep everyone involved. I've seen mediums focus on only one recipient and talk to that person in a quiet voice. It doesn't take long for the rest of the audience to lose interest, and then the energy in the room simply collapses.

The energy of everyone present is like a battery for you, and your goal is to stay fully charged, so a polished medium is cognizant of the whole room. You want all eyes on you, and you can only do that by including everyone. You can do this simply with the power of your voice. Even if you're speaking to only one person, make sure that your voice carries to everyone present.

Do your best not to ask questions of the recipient, other than to determine if they understand the evidence. Give them statements with confidence, as if there's no question in your mind that the information is correct. There are certain phrases you may use over and over to get across the information you're receiving. The following are some examples:

- I am aware that
- I sense
- I feel

- I'm hearing
- I'm seeing
- I'm cognizant of
- My attention is drawn to
- I'm mindful of
- It would seem from the impressions I'm receiving that
- I observe

There's a code of ethics that goes along with all demonstrations of mediumship. You should never pass along information that is too delicate to share in front of a group. You must be diligent to ensure that the evidence you provide from someone's loved ones doesn't hurt or embarrass them in public. For example, you may sense that a woman had an abortion. In a private session, there would be no problem talking about this, because it's just you and the sitter, but there's a fine line as to whether you mention this or not when others are around. In the case of someone who terminated a pregnancy, you could simply say, "You lost a baby early on," and leave it at that, or you could say nothing at all.

I once received evidence in a demonstration regarding the manner in which a murder was committed. Some of the information was appropriate to describe, but not all. I had to be careful not to upset the recipient of the message and very possibly the whole audience by going into sickening detail, no matter how evidential the information. You have a great responsibility to work in a manner that is respectable and that holds a high degree of ethics at all times.

No matter what type of information you receive, you'll have to be able to handle the situation if no one speaks up. This type of situation usually means that either someone in the audience isn't listening to you, or you haven't interpreted the information from the discarnate spirit the right way. I once gave a talk about mediumship at a Barnes and Noble bookstore. After the discussion I gave a demonstration. There was a large audience present, and I went directly to a woman in the first row.

"I have a woman in spirit who wishes to come to you," I said. "She appears to be your mother, her name is Helen, and she died suddenly of a heart attack at approximately sixty years old. There were no goodbyes. Is that correct?"

The woman shook her head and said she didn't know who I was talking about. I remember looking up at my spirit helpers and saying, "What are you doing?" Just then, a hand shot up right behind the woman I'd gone to. It was another woman, and she said, "That's my mother, and all the information you gave is correct." I then went on to give her the rest of the information I was sensing, and all of it was well received.

Not all demonstrations go perfectly. I gave another demonstration at a bookstore and things were going great, when this big guy stood and said, "You people are all going to Hell!"

I couldn't just ignore him, so I politely asked him to have a seat. That only made him more angry.

"You don't know the Bible!" he declared.

"I know the Bible better than you think," I said as politely as possible. "Jesus said we can do what he did. If you'd like to discuss it with me afterwards, I'll be happy to do so, but please don't disrupt this public demonstration."

He acted as if he didn't hear me and started quoting verses from the New Testament.

I told the man that his disruption wasn't fair to the other people there and asked him to take a seat. Luckily, he backed down, but not before someone called Security. Being confident in your abilities and being in charge of yourself and your audience will help in these types of situations.

In the off chance that you're very sure of what you're getting, but no one takes the evidence you're passing along, once again, fight your corner. The spirit who's come to you must belong to someone in the room. You can say something like, "I know someone here is not putting their hand up, so please see me afterwards." Many times I've given a demonstration and someone will come up to me afterwards to admit that they were too embarrassed to acknowledge my remarks. This can be frustrating, but it's part of doing public work.

In a group setting, most people in the room will sit there hoping you'll come to them. Unfortunately, in many cases there won't be time to satisfy everyone. Remember, this is a demonstration, not a reading for every person present. Just do the best you can and work with the information you're given from the spirit world. Trust that they know who needs to come through and are going to give you exactly what you and the audience need.

Public demonstrations allow for more variety than in private readings and can allow you to take mediumship to a higher level. I've brought in spirit artists like Rita Berkowitz and Joe Shiel to join me on the platform and draw the spirit communicator as I pass along evidence that I'm receiving at the same time. Talk about convincing!

Or consider the British medium Estelle Roberts ... She used to demonstrate for huge crowds at the Royal Albert Hall in London. Those lucky enough to be seated near her could actually hear the spirit world talking to her in an incredible example of direct independent voice.

That's the level of mediumship I'm always striving for. No matter where you are in your development, however, relax, and enjoy yourself. When you've worked hard at developing your skills and have become proficient at public demonstrations of mediumship, the whole audience will feel uplifted by your work.

There's no need to take yourself or your gifts completely seriously. From my years of training and working with some of the top mediums in Great Britain, I have to say that those people know how to have a rip-roaring good time with their work. They know they're good, and they show it, relaxing enough to be compassionate, when necessary, but also to laugh at the spirit world's humor when it comes through.

Pressure kills mediumship. If you feel yourself tensing up, make a conscious decision to let go and relax into your power. Just say, "Screw it! I'm going to have a good time with this!"

Whether serious or seriously funny, if the evidence you bring forward from your spirit communicators is highly evidential, everyone present in your public demonstration of mediumship will be in awe of it. That is what you want to strive for. Over and over reach a little higher for the most evidential details possible to reveal the continuity of life and to show that the love the spirit people had for those still here goes on.

Chapter 20
Living Intelligence

This book has focused on a specific type of communication with the other side: evidential mediumship. You've learned effective ways to show others the continuity of life by providing details that remove any doubt in the mind of the recipient that you are truly communicating with the spirit world. This is possible because a gifted, well-trained medium is not just attuning to static information, but is carrying on an active dialogue with living, thinking, intelligent spirit minds.

Note that I used the word "dialogue." Yes, mediums attune to the energy that's all around us, including the auras of the people to whom we give readings. Attuning to energy is a big part of what mediums do, but your messages will never open up to their full potential until you carry on an active conversation with the spirit world in real-time, attuning to information that is spirit-driven.

Throughout this book I have introduced to you the tools which will allow you to be the best medium you can be, but the most important aspect of your work, by far, is your rapport with living intelligence. During a reading or a public demonstration of mediumship, you open yourself as a conduit to the spirit world. There are endless possibilities to the information they can pass along through you, but being intelligent, they will always bring you exactly what they know is the best way to get their message across.

Imagine, for example, that you say to a woman, "I have a man named Bob here. He was 53 years old, he died of lung cancer, and he was a butcher." What happens if the woman says no to every detail? Because you're dealing with living intelligence, you can go back to the spirit world and mentally tell them, "She's saying no. Can you show me where to go with this?" And they do. This kind of rapport builds trust and confidence on both sides.

The spirit people want to help all of us. They want to help the people who come to you, and they want to help you do your work the best you can. They want to push you to higher levels, if you're willing to work with them. Their goal is the same as the goal of every good medium should be: to bring comfort. The ways in which they find to do that often blow me away.

I had a man come to me for a reading who had lost his child. He didn't tell me that himself, but his little girl came to me in spirit, accompanied by another family member on the other side. My heart broke for this man when his daughter showed me how she'd died: by being crushed under the wheels of the car he was driving. He hadn't known that she was behind him as he backed out of his driveway.

I went through the reading, giving him detail after detail that let him know I had his child, but I didn't know if the evidence I was passing along would be enough to change anything for him. The man's grief was palpable. I couldn't help but wonder how a person could live with something like that.

Then the little girl handled the situation all by herself. She put just the right words in my ear that her father needed to hear, and I passed them along. She said, "Dad, all you ever wanted to do was love me. You loved me so much."

Those words had an instant effect on the man. I could see them easing his guilt as I said them. The message showed the father that his daughter knew how much he cared for her and she knew that he would never have harmed her intentionally. "All you ever wanted to do was love me ..." It was such a simple message, yet I could never have thought of that myself—and that's my point: I didn't think of it. I didn't have to. That little girl was the perfect example of *living* intelligence.

In another prime example of the spirit world's ingenuity, I was giving a demonstration in my church one day when a young man came through showing me a pair of boots. I connected him with a woman in the congregation and learned in the course of the demonstration that the spirit communicator was the woman's son who had died in Iraq. I could see that the details were still quite painful for her, so as I often do when things get touchy in a public setting, I wrapped things up and later asked her to come and see me privately.

When the two of us sat down together alone, her son came through right away. What he showed me made me glad I hadn't continued on with the demonstration in church. This time he showed me how he'd thrown himself on a live grenade to save those around him. The mother cried and told me that she was furious at her husband for encouraging her son to join the military. I was able to pass along the soldier's very important message to his mother, thanks to having an active dialogue with him: that she shouldn't be mad at his father ... that he would have thrown himself on that grenade again if he had to.

I have to tell you, that young soldier impressed me beyond words. I wanted to stand up and salute him right there in my office. The connection with him was so clear that I could feel his patriotism and his sense of duty as if I were wearing a uniform myself. I'd never met this man, of course, yet I felt as if I knew him. As for me wanting to salute a spirit person? That's what you get when you're dealing with living intelligence.

Having that kind of interaction with the spirit world is very special. It's why I call this sacred work. It allows you to be exactly what a medium is supposed to be: an intermediary between this world and the next, and you can't have that kind of connection and work at that level unless you work very evidentially. For that, you have to take the information in this book very seriously. You have to do the exercises and sharpen your tools every chance you get. Being a credible medium takes years of dedicated work and practice, but your efforts will pay off in your increased rapport with the spirit world.

I'm sorry to say that when it comes to other-worldly things, there's a lot of nonsense being passed around these days, and the situation is exacerbated by the media. There's so much sensationalism on TV that's disrespectful to the spirit world. When they have shows about things like trapped souls and ghost whisperers, I can only shake my head and then work even harder at training more evidential mediums.

I don't believe in chaos. I believe that there is order to the universe. We come here to walk through this life to learn lessons, to accomplish things, and to grow. There are people in the spirit world helping us to do that, and it's not helpful to them when we believe otherwise.

If we come from intelligence as mediums, the types of things we see sensationalized on TV simply don't make sense. So much of what people see about the other side is hype and it preys on the minds of people who haven't been exposed to the reality of the spirit world. I have never met anything I should be afraid of in the spirit world. In all honesty, I should be much more afraid of the living! People here on the earth plane are the ones who create problems for us.

I've said this before and I'll say it now as we close this final chapter: You have to choose what kind of medium you want to be. Evidential mediumship is almost a lost art. I hear horror stories from my students all the time. One man told me how another medium said to him, "Be sure that when you demonstrate, that your messages are short and that you don't give too much information so they come back the next week." Another was told, "Proof of survival is neither important nor necessary" and "There's no reason to have evidence in mediumship."

I hope that—like me—when you read outrageous statements like that, they make you want to get out there and show the world what evidential mediumship is all about. Never settle for anything less than overwhelming people with evidence that you are communicating with a loving, intelligent spirit world.

You now have the knowledge and the tools to carry on in the tradition of some of the finest mediums in the world. Those who've gone before you have shined a light into the darkness and revealed the spirit world to those who needed most to see it.

So carry on. Choose to be the very best evidential medium you can be. Choose to be a keeper of the light.

Epilogue

As I walk through the path of my life, I know I have been given the God-given gift of being born a natural medium. Spiritually, mediumship has altered my perspective of God, the reason for our life here, and our continued existence as we go on from here. Standing for evidential mediumship has challenged me personally, particularly in opening my church and standing for our civil rights. If you are a medium, treasure your gift. Use it with integrity.

To paraphrase one of my favorite quotes: Spiritualism has been to me and to many others such a lifting of the mental horizons and letting in of the heavens that one can only compare it to sailing aboard a ship, living like a prisoner below deck with all of the hatches battened down. Then, suddenly one night, being allowed on deck for the first time, to the stupendous mechanism of the heavens all aglow with the glory of God.

Touch the hem of the spirit world with humility and awe. Dance your life to your song. Pray hard. Listen intently. Love greatly. Serve humanity. Be at peace, companion on the journey, be at peace.

In gratitude for the gift,

Janet

Appendix A
Sample Thank You Letters

The following are actual thank you letters I received from grateful clients. I include them here not out of pride, but to show you the kind of difference you can make in people's lives by practicing evidential mediumship.

I have changed some of the names and left out some of the personal details to protect the writer's privacy.

Dear Rev. Janet,

I could never thank you enough for what you have done for my family and I.

When my friend and I made the appointment to see you I was filled with the hopeful anticipation of perhaps "hearing" from my friend Sally who had passed suddenly in 1999. I believed that *she* would be surprised by the fact that there really is a life after the one we experience here. (She never believed it in life). Sally and I had been so close for so long I felt sure that if it were at all possible, she would be there and would have something to say. I could never have imagined how surprised *I* was going to be.

You looked right at me in a room of 10 people, described my father, his name, his illness, and the circumstances surrounding his death as if you had been there. You said that he was very assertive, and very insistent (just like my dad) ... that he needed to say that he was very sorry. He also said that it was very important that I tell the kids. I was stunned. If you had only said this about my father it would have been amazing, but you went on to describe my father holding an infant (My older brother died just weeks after his birth). You mentioned the names of people who were very important to my father (I barely remembered these people at all, and only after you mentioned them by name. These people were my father's best friends in life). You mentioned my maternal grandmother and the grandson who was named after him. You said that my dad was concerned about the grandson who was named after him. None of this was what I wanted to hear. It was exactly what I had needed to hear.

After the demonstration, I talked with my family about the information you gave me. We cried together and tried to figure out why our father would say that he was sorry to us. We then examined our own lives, with regard to our own children and our expectations of them. It was suddenly very obvious to us that we could never hold our children responsible for our decisions about how we live, where we live, or our decisions regarding our healthcare. We all agreed that absolutely nothing could cause us to stop loving our children.

In the light that you provided, my burden of guilt (over my father) dissolved like cotton candy in warm water. It is impossible to convey the scope of this cathartic and healing experience in words. All I can say is thank you, for all of us, thank you.

With deepest gratitude,

(Name withheld)

Dearest Janet,

My husband and I had a reading with you a few weeks back and I had to write to tell you that your reading was life-changing for both of us ...

My husband lost a beautiful daughter in a car crash which has haunted him ever since. Through your ability to reach across to the other side he knows without a doubt that her spirit lives on!! He dreams of her and knows that she is fine and happy. The peace he feels now is just remarkable, thanks to you and your blessed gift.

As for myself, my childhood was very, very painful. My mother came through and gave me the most precious gift she could ever have: an apology, followed by a confirmation that my experience was not imagined ... that she "had a lot of regret where I was concerned." I will never forget those words. The internal shift inside me was astounding.

Thank you, Janet. You are truly remarkable and a gift. Keep doing God's work and I will see you in the future, my friend.

Much love and blessings and gratitude,

(Name withheld)

Dear Janet,

Five years ago I walked into the Wiseman Bookstore to buy an angel pin for my mother-in-law who was dying from cancer. I walked past a room set up with chairs and a podium and felt myself drawn to this room. When I asked what the room was used for, I was told it was set up for a Spiritualist church. I decided two weeks later to attend a service.

I was having difficulty finding joy in my life at this time, especially after the loss of two close friends who had died within a week of each other, nine months prior, and now my mother-in-law's battle with cancer.

I was attending my second service when you asked if you could come to me with a message. I said yes, not knowing what to expect but willing to listen. The message was clearly from my friend who as I mentioned before died nine months before. The details you gave me regarding him fit so perfectly. I was in shock as well as amazement that anyone could know all these things, but at the same time a feeling of peace washed over me.

My belief and understanding of mediumship has grown significantly over the past five years. I have been able to make some sense out of people's passing, knowing that although I can't see and touch them in the physical sense, that they hear and see all.

I have since lost my dad, with whom my relationship could be somewhat difficult at times, especially in my earlier years. When I started getting messages from him, his love became ever more evident than it had been years before and I was able to see things more clearly with regards to our relationship. That knowledge has given me self-love and self-worth. It has made me look at life differently, more objectively and with a greater passion for things. It has taught me to react differently to my family and believe in love as our greatest gift.

Thank God, and thank you, Janet.

(Name withheld)

Appendix B
Sample Transcript of a Reading

The following is the verbatim transcript of a private reading, given over the phone, proving that a medium doesn't have to be in the presence of the sitter to give an outstanding reading. My words are in normal script. The sitter's words are in italics:

There's a gentleman here who was pretty sick… why would I be thinking about black lung condition? Who would have worked where black lung would have been an issue… around coal… a manual job where they would have been around…

You're talking about my father. He used to shovel coal on steam engines when he first started working for the railroad.

I sensed that your dad died around a holiday or somebody's birthday.

He died the day after his mother's birthday.

He must have had heart problems… he keeps hitting my heart, so there must have been heart problems.

Yes, he did.

Are you the only girl or the baby girl? Why would your dad make you very important? Were you close with your dad? Because he keeps talking about that – he makes you very important.

I was the baby, and we were especially close.

He keeps wanting to show me ships or boats… I don't know why. Any naval connection? I don't know why he's showing me boats.

Yes, I spent 20 years in the Navy.

This definitely comes through the way a father would come. Someone wrote some kind of poem or a letter at the end. There's something there that he's acknowledging that it's very, very important to him.

Yes! My brother wrote a poem about him the week he died.

Do you have a connection to Virginia?

I'm calling you from Virginia. (The area code was from a phone in Florida)

Get outta here! If you're there now, then your dad knows exactly where you are, because I wouldn't know that.

He must have known a lot of people – there was a huge response to him when he passed.

My mother's gotten all kinds of cards.

Your mother is digging her heels in about something. She doesn't want to do something? Why are you supposed to back off your mother? Why am I supposed to tell you not to push your mother? Either that or she hasn't come full circle to deal with something… it keeps coming up. Show me one more time…

I don't know…

This was pretty recent. This is not an old passing.

Yes. He died just two months ago.

It feels pretty recent. There's something about William… or Bill…

That's his name! Bill!

Your dad is okay.

I knew he would be, but he didn't believe in an afterlife.

He loved you, and that would transfigure everything, when they know that's the way to your heart. He's okay.

He had a big dog … There was a black lab or chocolate lab.

Not that I know of.

Yes there was. It might have been a dog when he was growing up. Definitely. Remember I said this. (Note: This was later confirmed by the man's widow, who said he was crazy about his big black Doberman)

He was actually kind of a charming man.

Oh, yes. Definitely.

I want to say that about him. Personality continues.

There's somebody like Dotty or Delores or David, something with a D…

I don't know who that would be.

Just think about that. Was one of your grandmothers kind of smaller? There's a petite woman here behind him.

His mother was kind of short.

I'm supposed to tell you about a cardinal bird. That would be a sign that he wants you to know he's around. I think there's a little nudge. (Note that later a cardinal appeared while the sitter's family was visiting the hospice where Bill died. The bird landed on the roof of his room and stayed there).

Your mother must be talking to a picture of him.

Yes, I think she is.

Because I'm supposed to tell her that he hears her all the time. I don't know if she put his ring on or she's holding his ring… it's very significant to him. He brought that up.

She is wearing his ring behind hers!

She could not have changed this. Is your mother somewhat health conscious? She's beating herself up that she could have done more, and your mom couldn't have done more.

I do think she's feeling some guilt.

When it's your time, it's your time. It's very important for him, because she really is going over and over that event and she couldn't have taken better care of him.

I'll be sure to tell her.

Your dad's talking about someone else who died tragically who wasn't that old… I felt quickness. Why do I have to go back a couple of years?

Oh, God. That's my step-daughter, who was killed by lightning two years ago. She was 27.

Let me go on and ask her.

She had longer hair. You have shorter hair, not like hers.

Yes.

There was some delay with something when she died. About someone finding out? Delay… delay…

My husband and I were out of the country. Nobody could find us for two days to give us the news.

Who's Crissy? Chris.. I don't know if it's a friend of hers…

That's her friend from high school who was killed by a drunk driver!

Yeah. She's gotten to see her on the other side.

I don't know why, but I want to say something about Poo – or a nick-name like Poo… Like peek-a-boo.

That was a nickname they called her dad!

Oh, that's a good validation that it's her.

There's something about 17 or 18. Anything happen around January 8th? 7th or 8th or 17th or 18th?

That doesn't ring a bell.

Think about it later.

Show me again… show me in a different way.

There's something L. She keeps showing someone with L.

Liam?

Yeah. Who's that?

That's her unborn son. She was six months pregnant when she died.

Any Irish in your family? Why's she showing me St. Patrick's Day? Might be another date when something happened.

Liam is an Irish name.

Not too long before she passed there was some kind of big, I don't know… wedding anniversary or party or something…

She was married just 7 months before she died.

She has a sibling – she's indicating someone to her side, which would be a sibling, and there's something about the month of August.

She had one sister, but I'm not sure about the August connection.

She's saying, "It's not her fault," about when she died.

That's true.

And she's showing me something about a blue uniform.

She was a sergeant in the Marine Corps. She was buried in her dress blues.

She always wanted to take care of people… take care of kids, and I think this is part of what she's doing on the other side.

That would absolutely be her.

She just wants everybody to know she's ok.   Is this your hus-band's daughter?

Yes.

Does he still carry her picture when she was younger? There's some-thing about a picture of her when she was younger… with him. I almost think he carries it.

I'll have to check.

Now your dad is stacking coins on my desk. Like silver dollars ... half dollars...it's either a coin or a medal. Like a buffalo nickel... ask your mom.

Oh my gosh! I was just at my parents house and my mother and I found this big buffalo nickel, but we didn't know what it was. It was a belt buckle. And my mother found a stack of silver dollars, just like you said.

Show me one more time... He's going to come to you in some kind of dream if you already haven't had it. It's not a dream, it's an actual visit from him. It's not a dream.

I sense that he was picky about his shoes. There's something about his shoes. I don't know what that's about, but it's very important to him.

His feet swelled up at the end and there was only one pair he could wear.

Do you have a sister?

Yes.

Is she in the middle of changing stuff around, like fixing something in the house?

I'll have to check.

He wants her to know he's there with her....

Your parents used to dance.

Yes.

Did your mom play the piano?

Yes. In their later years they both enjoyed playing.

I'm getting Art Linkletter. And your dad played football.

I think so. In high school.

There's an old photo with a 9 or 19 or 29. Was he into sports at all? I'm sure about this.

I'll ask my mother.

He had a brother.

Yes.

It's either a picture of your dad with that shirt on, or it's your dad next to his brother with that shirt on with a 9 on it – or it's your dad with a sweater on with a 9 or 19 or 29. Ask your mother.

I will.

How long's he been gone?

Two months.

Yeah, he'll get stronger (at sending signals). There was nothing anybody could do. It was his time to go.

What? ... I'm still talking to him ...

There's something about those coins again. I don't know if it's half dollars or buffalo nickels. He's okay.

Do you have any questions?

Yes. Since he didn't believe in life after death, is he surprised that there's more?

(Pause) He says it's like an "aha" moment, so I don't know that I want to say "surprised." It's almost like he feels contentment.

Is your mom on her own?

Yes.

Is she going to stay that way for a while?

Yes.

She needs her space. You shouldn't push her to be closer ... Your mom's not sleeping so good.

That's right.

He's around. This is a validation to her that he's around, because he knows she's not resting well. She couldn't have done anything to help him. She took really good care of him.

Well, that's what I got.

Janet, that was fantastic. Thank you so much. I can't wait to share this with my family. What a gift you have.